A CARING PRESENCE

Dear Jim—
thanks for being
"A CARING PRESENCE"
IN my life!
IN friendship—
THe Rabbi... (Matzah!)

Rabbi [signature]

Rabbi Simeon Schreiber

A Caring Presence

Bringing the Gift of Hope, Comfort and Courage

**Guidelines for Visiting
Hospital Patients
The Homebound Elderly
Shivah/Bereaved Family**

gefen גפן
publishing house בית הוצאה לאור
JERUSALEM • NEW YORK
Est. 1981

Excerpt in appendix II reproduced from *Making Sense of Suffering: A Jewish Approach* by Yitzchok Kirzner, with permission from the copyright holders, Artscroll/Mesorah Publications, Ltd.

Cover Design: Michal Cohen
Typesetting: David Yehoshua

ISBN: 978-965-229-557-6

1 3 5 7 9 8 6 4 2

Gefen Publishing House Ltd.
6 Hatzvi Street
Jerusalem 94386, Israel
972-2-538-0247
orders@gefenpublishing.com

Gefen Books
11 Edison Place
Springfield, NJ 07081
1-800-477-5257
orders@gefenpublishing.com

www.gefenpublishing.com

Printed in Israel   *Send for our free catalogue*

Library of Congress Cataloging-in-Publication Data

Schreiber, Simeon.
A caring presence : bringing the gift of hope, comfort and courage : guidelines for visiting hospital patients, the homebound elderly, shiva/bereaved family / Simeon Schreiber.
p. cm.

ISBN 978-965-229-557-6

1. Visiting the sick (Judaism) 2. Consolation (Judaism) 3. Jewish mourning customs. I. Title.
BM729.V5S37 2011   •   296.6'1--dc23   •   2011034176

אֵשֶׁת־חַיִל מִי יִמְצָא, וְרָחֹק מִפְּנִינִים מִכְרָהּ.

בָּטַח בָּהּ לֵב בַּעְלָהּ, וְשָׁלָל לֹא יֶחְסָר....

כַּפָּהּ פָּרְשָׂה לֶעָנִי, וְיָדֶיהָ שִׁלְּחָה לָאֶבְיוֹן....

פִּיהָ פָּתְחָה בְחָכְמָה, וְתוֹרַת חֶסֶד עַל־לְשׁוֹנָהּ....

רַבּוֹת בָּנוֹת עָשׂוּ חָיִל, וְאַתְּ עָלִית עַל־כֻּלָּנָה....

An accomplished woman, who can find? Her value is far beyond pearls.

Her husband's heart relies on her and he shall lack no fortune....

She spreads her palm to the poor and extends her hand to the destitute....

She opens her mouth with wisdom and a lesson of kindness is upon

her tongue....

Many daughters have achieved greatly, but you have surpassed them all....

(EXCERPTED FROM PROVERBS 31)

This book is dedicated with deep gratitude and appreciation by

Mr. Joseph Sirotkin

in honor of his devoted wife

Beverly

For more than sixty-three years Beverly has been his friend, confidante, and soul mate, giving him unconditional love, unwavering support, and unbounded loyalty.

Truly, through her commitment, she has earned the right to wear the crown of *aishet chayil* with pride.

In the merit of all of their noble deeds of charity and acts of kindness, may God bless Joseph and Beverly Sirotkin with many more years of physical health, spiritual tranquility, and the serenity of true *shalom*, peace, in every facet of their lives.

Contents

Foreword

The young man was just twenty-four years old when he decided to move to Israel to complete his master's degree in Near Eastern studies at Tel Aviv University. He had another dream as well: to serve in the armed forces of Israel, a country he deeply loved and admired.

When the letter arrived from the army medical office requesting that he return to their office immediately, he was elated and euphoric. His dream was about to come true. But he was not immediately accepted. He was told that he needed another set of chest X-rays because something didn't look right. "No time to waste," they said, so he complied immediately. The doctor who read the X-rays was blunt in his diagnosis. In a cold Germanic voice he said, "You have lymphoma. You will need chemotherapy. You will throw up a lot. Your hair will fall out. But you will be okay. You will have to be a man!"

The young man began to cry. Suddenly, he was no longer an aspiring soldier. He was a frightened child in desperate need of his father.

The young man was my son Jacob.

Within three days of his diagnosis, I had him back in the United States, ready to undergo a battery of tests. Ultimately, we learned that he had developed Hodgkin's disease, a sometimes fatal but often curable cancer.

And so began my involvement with the *mitzvah* of *bikur cholim* – the selfless and rewarding act of caring for others who are physically ill or emotionally distressed. Jacob struggled and, thank God, survived.

(In fact, he is married and the father of a beautiful family!) In the process, we both learned a good deal about the mindset of illness and what visitors should and should not do.

Visiting those who are ill is a universal tradition, an act of kindness that is not reserved exclusively for the Jewish people. Every day, people of all nationalities and religious and spiritual persuasions visit their loved ones at home, in hospitals, or in nursing facilities, with the hope of bringing comfort and solace to them. Visiting the sick demonstrates that someone *cares* about someone else's well-being. It is an act of compassion that is always appreciated and never forgotten. Its motivation, however, is *personal* and derives from deep feelings of one individual for another.

The Jewish concept of visiting the ill – *bikur cholim* – is distinctly different: though it certainly can create personal benefit, its true mandate, according to the twelfth-century philosopher Maimonides, is the fulfillment of one of the principles written in the Torah, to "love thy neighbor as thyself" (Leviticus 19:18). This is because, in a deeper sense, it furthers *tikkun olam:* repairing the world and making it a better place in which to live. Viewed in this way, its focus is no longer on the individual; it is on the community. A healthy and spiritual community will be the catalyst for a better world for all of us.

But irrespective of its rationale, at its core is the fact that visiting the sick is a *mitzvah*, a good deed, a Torah instruction that can be performed by every individual.

As with many laws and customs in the Torah, there are both proper and improper ways to perform this *mitzvah*. Understandably, for many individuals, the fulfillment of *bikur cholim* is uncomfortable. When to visit, how long to stay, what to say, what topics to avoid, how to act in the presence of someone who is ill – these are just a few of the areas of concern. It is my hope that this book, *A Caring Presence*, will provide the answers to these questions and many more.

It will attempt to answer what *bikur cholim* is and what it is not. The Biblical and Talmudic sources for the performance of *bikur cholim* will be discussed, sometimes utilizing novel approaches and interpretations. It will address what the *mitzvah* accomplishes for you, the visitor, as well as the patient. You will also learn about the many and varied emotions that the person you are visiting possibly may be experiencing and how to respond to them.

Through a scripted scenario, you will be taken on a "virtual" hospital visit. You will review the visit point by point and determine which of the visitor's actions you consider proper and which improper. Then we will review the visit together and develop twenty-one guidelines for effective visits.

Finally, I will attempt to develop a meaningful insight: a theological response to patients who are suffering and feel that God does not hear them, that He is not listening to their prayers or has abandoned them.

It is my hope that you will read and reread this book until you are comfortable with its messages and advice. Its content is not meant to be inflexible or written in stone. It is intended strictly as a guide that can be amended according to your needs and abilities.

It is my prayer that ultimately this book will help you transform what may have been for you an uncomfortable *mitzvah* into one that is comfortable. May it bring you unbounded joy and result in unimaginable rewards to your spirit and soul.

Acknowledgments

I never expected to write a book! Although I had given numerous lectures to groups of men and women who were interested in forming *bikur cholim* visitation groups, it never occurred to me to convert these lectures into a written document until a friend suggested that my presentation material could really serve as a basis for a book. I was reluctant, but I have three wonderful friends who unknowingly influenced me to attempt it.

When they see their names in this acknowledgement, they probably will be shocked. But, unbeknownst to them, I greatly admire their tenacity of spirit, their energy, their refusal to let life pass by without tasting every morsel, their ability to make every moment in their lives count. They inspire those around them to try, to do, to accomplish.

To these three special friends – **Morton Landowne**, **Steven Spira**, and **Dr. Alan Helfer** – I say thank you for giving me the motivation to emulate each of you.

About eighteen years ago, I had the good fortune to meet an "energy machine" who has been a dear friend and an astute listener, someone who has continually encouraged me to work on this project. I am forever grateful to this wonderful woman: **Dr. Ruth Westheimer**.

There are others who have been at my side as the ideas began to take shape: **Edie Shapiro**, Director of Volunteer Services at Mount Sinai Medical Center in Florida, who has been such a special friend and confidante who has always provided a compassionate and listening ear; and **Jonnie Vargas,** who has typed and retyped so many letters, speeches, and manuscripts, never complaining about the workload. And what would I do without **Joelle Silverman Miller**, the creator of By Design Communications, whom I was blessed to meet eight years ago? Without her, I never would have attempted this project. The word *time* doesn't exist in Joelle's vocabulary. No matter what time of day or night, Joelle has always been there for me – reading, editing, suggesting, typing. What can I say but thank you, thank you.

A symphony orchestra needs a conductor – a maestro who melds the musicians with their instruments to produce the melodic composition intended by the composer. An editor is certainly no less than a maestro. How fortunate I am to have had **Charlotte Friedland** as my capable and brilliant editor. Her ability to change a word, substitute a phrase, or suggest an idea was invaluable in the development of this book. My appreciation for her remarkable talent is boundless.

Publisher **Ilan Greenfield** immediately expressed his belief that my manuscript would be a valuable contribution to the Jewish community. I am deeply grateful to his excellent staff at **Gefen Publishing House**, particularly editor **Kezia Raffel Pride**, for the careful and competent production of this book.

Seven years ago, when the skies of my life suddenly and unexpectedly became darkened, a heavenly "rainbow" appeared on the horizon. It became, and continues to be, a never-ending source of support, encouragement, caring, and friendship. Although anonymous by choice, it is this colorful rainbow that has never stopped providing all manner of support, for which I am eternally grateful. May you continue to always shine brightly and bring light, warmth, and hope to all who admire and love you.

I have always wanted to be an inspiration to my children and grandchildren – to leave them (after 120 years) with some legacy, some accomplishment, that they could point to in my life that would add meaning and purpose to their lives as well. I hope that my example of doing for others, whether materially or by community service, will be remembered and, hopefully, emulated by each of my wonderful, loving, and gifted children of whom I am so tremendously proud: **Paula Lev and her husband Mark; Jacob Schreiber and his wife Edna; Miriam Skydell and her husband Jamie; David Schreiber and his wife Laurie, Nachum Schwartz and his wife Ilene**. Of course, my heartfelt love and gratitude go to their offspring, my grandchildren, **Joshua, Alex, Jillian; Gavri, Maya, Simi-Tal; Nicole, Andrew, Brian, Jordan; Jeremy, Ami, Aviva, and Jocelyn**.

If one is fortunate in life, one can sometimes "connect the dots"… connect events of the past with outcomes of the present. I strongly believe that God has a Hand in our destiny and that there is a reason for every occurrence in our lives: if in the present we could just see into the future, we would realize that everything that happens always happens for a reason.

I met **my wife, Rose,** more than thirty years ago on a remote island in Puerto Rico during a Passover holiday celebration. She had no plans to be there, but chose it only after she threw some darts on a dartboard map in an attempt to select a place to be for the holiday. Luckily, the dart stuck to Puerto Rico. We were seated, "by chance," at the same table in the dining room: the rest is history. Rose taught me the value of giving and has constantly encouraged my involvement in serving the community. She was relentless in pushing me to continue my writing – even though I often felt that I would not be able to complete this project. Her desire for me to succeed encouraged, inspired, and motivated me to continue. I hope I have made her proud.

No list of acknowledgement would be complete without giving thanks to God, Who has "kept me alive, sustained me, and allowed me to come to this time." I've often thought that, strange as it may seem, were it not for the fact that more than twenty years ago my son Jacob discovered that he had cancer, I probably never would have thought about *bikur cholim*, caring for others, doing for others, the concept of chaplaincy, or of writing this book. But I believe that there is and there was a plan – one that I did not understand at the time and one that I would not, given the choice, want to repeat. But God controls the world and our destinies. From bad, there can be good – that is why we make a blessing and thank God not only when "good" things happen, but for the "bad" occurrences as well. Who knows, maybe what we consider "bad" turns out in the end to be "good"?

And so, I acknowledge and give thanks to the One and Only God, who is involved on a daily basis in each of our lives. He sometimes does things that we do not understand or agree with, but we are not God and cannot comprehend Him. What we can understand is that we live here through His grace and His permission.

May You, dear God, continue to bestow Your blessings upon the people and the land of Israel and grant us all health, happiness, contentment, and *shalom* – peace.

PART I
HOSPITAL VISITS

Chapter One

Defining *Bikur Cholim:* A Few Surprises!

Bikur cholim is *not* about helping those who are, unfortunately, ill or in emotional distress. "Helping" implies that there are two categories of people: the Helpers, who are the heroes, performing acts of kindness and compassion out of the goodness of their hearts, and the Needy, who are less fortunate, and therefore beholden to the selfless Helpers. To think in this two-category characterization only exacerbates the feelings of helplessness and dependency that sufferers of illness are already experiencing. There is no value in further fostering these negative feelings, which can become debilitating for the individual.

I prefer to define the act of *bikur cholim* as "being of service" to one's fellow human being. This is an important distinction. When one person is of service to another, both individuals are on the same level, and their interactions must always retain this necessary balance. True, one is healthy and one may be ill. However, serving someone not because it's a nice thing to do, but motivated rather by the principles of caring, respect, and love for another human being – another of God's holy creations – promotes equality in the relationship.

Much like the principle of charity, which in Hebrew is called *tzedakah*, righteousness, the motivation is *not* because we are nice people doing a good deed for those less fortunate, but because it is the right and the just thing to do. We act *not* from a personal perspective and a subjective value system, but from the moral and ethical teachings and values mandated by a higher Authority.

The Hebrew word for service is *avodah*. Contained within this word is a three-letter root, *eved*, which means servant. Only one individual in the Torah was called "God's servant" (*eved Hashem*), and that person was Moses.

Do you recall Moses' first encounter with God? In the book of Exodus (3:1–5), the Bible tells us that Moses was a shepherd and that he suddenly came upon an eye-catching phenomenon: a "burning bush" that was somehow not consumed by the fire. What was God's first requirement of Moses? What was His first instruction? Before God would dialogue with Moses, He commanded him, "Take off your shoes, for the place upon which you are standing is holy."

How strange! Why should Moses have to remove his shoes? What purpose could there be in doing that? I propose that the reason was to teach Moses a lesson, one that he would need to utilize his entire life as he led and served the Jewish people: when one is barefoot, he immediately feels and senses the ground – its contour, its texture, its temperature, the pebbles, the stones. In a word, he becomes *sensitive* to his surroundings. Aren't these the very qualities and requisites necessary for leadership and service? To be aware of and sensitive to the feelings, to the emotions, to the pain and heartache of the individual one is serving? Aren't these same qualities of sensitivity and caring exactly the essential requirements of those engaged in the act of *bikur cholim*?

And so, our mission in performing this act of kindness is to *serve* our fellow human beings as we would want to be served ourselves.

We must learn not only to listen to what is being said, but to *hear* it as well. We must not only be touched by their troubles and concerns, we must feel and internalize them as well.

This formula for the interaction between human beings – where equality promotes dignity and self-esteem – is truly the ultimate act of service to both God and His creations.

Although the term *bikur cholim* is thought by many to mean "visiting the sick," surprisingly, we do not find *bikur* defined as "visiting" anywhere in rabbinic literature. What, then, does *bikur* really mean?

In the Hebrew language, spellings are not accidental or inconsequential. By reconfiguring the Hebrew letters that spell the word *bikur*, we can create the word *boker*, which means dawn or early morning – a time when the darkness of the night begins to wane and the light of a new day begins to shine.

People who are ill or in emotional distress often experience feelings of darkness – of fear, anxiety, loneliness, and despair. Alone with their emotions, isolated from others, there is often a feeling of abandonment, that there is no one to hear them, that there is no one able to help them.

The visitor who performs the compassionate *mitzvah* of *bikur cholim* can provide the antidote to these feelings. By visiting the ill, we bring those who are in the darkness of loneliness and despair the hope and the light of a new day, the reassurance that they are not alone, that there is someone who cares for them, someone who will listen to their concerns and fears and be with them in their time of need. Understood in this way, *boker* means the shining of light, the warmth and glow of its rays, the promise and the hope of new and better circumstances.

King David writes in Psalm 27, "One thing I ask of the Lord and this is my plea: to dwell in the House of the Lord all the days of my life and to visit [*u'le'vaker*] His sanctuary." King David's request seems to be problematic. If one is already dwelling in the House of the Lord, why express a separate request to "visit" one part of it?

In his book titled *Seventy Faces: Articles of Faith*, Rabbi Norman Lamm suggests a beautiful response to the apparent confusion in Psalm 27. *Le'vaker*, he states, derives its true meaning, as we have just noted, from the word *boker* – dawn or light. It does not mean, as generally assumed, "to visit." Rather, King David is praying for "the ability...to bring light and dawn and joy into the Temple so that others who worship with him will find their lives transformed and filled with a new light and reason to live."[1]

This is the true essence of *bikur cholim*: one's mere "caring presence" – just being there, a selfless expression of compassion by one individual toward another – is transformative. It can bring hope and joy with the faith and promise of a better and brighter tomorrow.

---

1. Norman Lamm, *Seventy Faces: Articles of Faith*, vol. 2 (Hoboken, NJ: Ktav, 2002).

Chapter Two

If You Are Uncomfortable in a Hospital/Nursing Home Setting

I was approached by a group of young professionals, men and women who were interested in forming a *bikur cholim* hospital visitation group. They were all accomplished in their occupations, but felt that something was missing in their lifestyles. They felt that they were spending their lives "taking from others" but not giving back, and the emptiness they felt, despite their material success, was creating anxiety and frustration. They wanted to redirect their lifestyles onto a path that would give them some spiritual satisfaction and put their values into practice.

Before the initial meeting began, a young lady approached me and asked whether she could speak to me privately – she had a very personal concern that needed to be addressed prior to her taking part in the formation of this group. She began speaking slowly and then tears began rolling down from her blue eyes.

"I want so much to try to bring comfort to those who are ill. But," she continued, "my mother died in a hospital after suffering for many months. I was so helpless... I was so incapable of helping her, of doing or saying something to ease her pain. I'm afraid that the memory of her suffering will debilitate me and make it impossible for me to visit anyone ever again. Is it possible to be an 'inactive' visitor?"

The answer to this question lies in just how we define the *mitzvah* and the physical act of visiting the sick as well as the true purpose of the visit.

We are taught that the Torah contains 613 *mitzvot* (commandments). Of this total, 365 are negative directives (such as "You shall not steal," "You shall not commit murder") while 248 are positive directives (such as "Honor your father and mother," and "Keep the Sabbath"). Because many of the commandments enumerated in the Torah are no longer applicable to us today (such as those that require the existence of the *Beit Hamikdash*, the Holy Temple in Jerusalem, for their fulfillment), we are not able to perform them.

What about *bikur cholim*? The sources for this *mitzvah* are discussed in appendix I, but for now, we are concerned with its practical application. Is it an act of kindness that everyone is able to perform? Is it an obligation for those individuals who are unable to enter a medical facility because of physical, emotional, or psychological reasons? What about individuals who are unable to deal with the sights, sounds, and smells associated with hospital or nursing home settings? What about those whose loved ones passed away in a hospital or nursing home, and the memories are too much to bear? Are these individuals exempt from the *mitzvah* of *bikur cholim*, or must they fulfill the *mitzvah* even though it means suffering and enduring personal discomfort?

Let us examine the essence of *bikur cholim* – its true meaning and purpose – before we attempt to answer these questions.

The Talmud (Shabbat 127a) records the following: "These are the actions that one can perform, and by so doing gain for oneself the dividends of these acts in this world, while retaining the principal for his benefit in the afterlife." Nine deeds are enumerated:

(1) Honoring one's father and mother
(2) Performing deeds of kindness
(3) Early attendance at the house of study, morning and evening
(4) Hospitality to guests, especially strangers
(5) Visiting the sick
(6) Dowering the bride
(7) Escorting the dead
(8) Concentration during prayer
(9) Bringing peace between man and his fellow man, as well as between husband and wife

As noted, the fifth *mitzvah* is *bikur cholim*. Returning to our original question, one might argue that the reason there are nine *mitzvot* listed is to make certain that one's reward in the afterlife is guaranteed even if one is unable to perform all of them. The individual who is unable, for the reasons enumerated previously, to visit someone who is ill would not be required to do so and would, in effect, be "excused" from the *mitzvah* of *bikur cholim*, but could still rely on the other eight *mitzvot* as merits.

This conclusion would be valid only if we define the act of *bikur cholim* according to the popularly accepted definition, i.e., physically visiting the sick. In truth, however, this definition is inaccurate and flawed. The reality is that *bikur cholim* has many facets. The *mitzvah* itself is like an umbrella with many spokes that not only keep it open but give more support and additional strength to it as well.

Indeed, the *mitzvah* of *bikur cholim* is not limited to physical visitation. It can be accomplished in a variety of ways and through multiple acts of kindness, including sending a card or letter that expresses the hope and prayer that the individual will have a complete and speedy recovery, or making a telephone call to the patient or family expressing concern for the individual's well-being and healing. (Note: telephone callers or text messagers should not ask for a return phone call or update. Remember, patients are ill and families are tired after a long day of caregiving. Your sincere interest is more important than their response.)

Making sure that the patient's personal and familial needs are addressed is another way of performing the *mitzvah* of *bikur cholim*. Stocking the refrigerator with food, making certain the house is kept neat and clean during the patient's absence, sending meals to the family (especially for Shabbat), providing transportation for the family to and from the hospital, even caring for their pets – these are just some of the things one can do to fulfill the mandate of *bikur cholim*.

Think creatively! You will find that with so many meaningful ways of servicing those who are ill, *bikur cholim* becomes one of the easiest *mitzvot* – even if you are unable to visit the patient physically.

The young lady who had approached me with her personal concern was transformed by this simple explanation. She became a leader in the group and created, developed, and organized many alternative visiting options. Now that she was able to perform the *mitzvah* of *bikur cholim* without ever setting foot in a hospital, her life became imbued with new meaning and direction.

Chapter Three

The Visitor's Role:

What It *Is*, What It Is *Not*

My awakening came quickly and without warning.

It was during my first year of internship, when I was taking courses at New York University Hospital in clinical pastoral education toward a degree as a hospital chaplain. One of the patients to whom I was assigned that day was an elderly gentleman who, I was told, didn't want to live any longer. During our talk, I found out that he had been a successful accountant, had four children, seven grandchildren, and would soon celebrate his sixty-fifth wedding anniversary. His life had been good, he said, but he was tired of living, of merely existing.

I was determined to change his mind about wanting to die. It would be simple, a "no-brainer." Using my limited knowledge of accounting terminology, I argued that he was only focusing on the debits in his life. "Look at all the credits you have: a wife, a family, children, and grandchildren, and a sixty-fifth wedding celebration on the horizon! You have not balanced your books properly!"

He nodded his apparent approval and five minutes later, I left his room. I was elated. I was patting myself on the back: job well done, you're on your way to becoming a successful chaplain!

Two days later, I was approached by the patient's wife and daughter. He was again feeling depressed and they were worried about him. Since I had been such a help a few days ago, would I revisit him? "Of course," I replied. "No problem."

As I entered the room, the patient took one look at me and a stream of expletives shot from his mouth! "Get out of here! Get out!" he shouted repeatedly.

I was stunned. Never had I expected such a reception, especially after I had been so successful initially. I almost ran from the room, immediately looked for my supervisor, and told her what happened. "What did I do to deserve such a response?" I asked. "We got along so well last time."

Her answer has stayed with me all of my professional life. "It's not what you did," she said. "It's what you did *not* do. You didn't hear a word he said. You listened to his words, but you didn't *hear* them. You were focused on yourself. You were so intent on changing his mood and changing his outlook that you missed the point. He just wanted to be heard, to be validated. Remember: you are a chaplain – that is your title. You are not 'Mr. Fix-It.'"

By nature, most of us like to "fix" a problem; it makes us feel good to know that we've solved a troublesome situation, that we've restored a sense of calm and balance to what was once a difficult and unsettling set of circumstances. In our minds, we want to be the knight who comes charging in on a white horse, rescues the struggling princess, and gallops off into the sunset.

Unfortunately, those who are engaged in the *mitzvah* of *bikur cholim* do not have a magic pill that always makes things better. Moreover, even if we possessed some magical powers, it is not the role or the responsibility of the *bikur cholim* visitor to change the circumstances or alleviate the condition of the person who is suffering. We cannot cure the person of his illness and we cannot reverse the deadly process of a terminal illness.

What, then, is our role? What is expected of us when we visit a patient? Perhaps we can learn what our role is by first defining what it is *not*.

- We are *not* there to render medical advice.
- We are *not* there to compare our own current or past illnesses to the ones they are experiencing.
- We are *not* there to change their situation.
- We are *not* there to take away their illness and suffering.
- We are *not* there to make them laugh at our jokes.
- And surprisingly, we are *not* necessarily there to make them happy.

After eliminating so many possibilities from our repertoire, what is our role as visitors and caregivers? The role of the *bikur cholim* visitor can be formulated into three basic categories.

1. *Determine where the patient is emotionally.* The visitor's role is to be with the patient in his time of suffering and distress. We must learn to listen not only to what he is saying, but to focus our attention and to *hear* him as well. We are to search for the words behind the music to determine his state of mind. What is he truly feeling, despite outward signs of calmness and serenity?

One of the most difficult disciplines for visitors to learn is the ability to simply listen, to allow the patient to talk, to unburden his troubled soul. God provided us with two ears and one mouth –

perhaps to remind us that we should listen twice as much as we speak! "*Shema Yisrael*," the declaration of our Jewish belief in one God, begins with the word *Shema*, hear. *Listen* to what is being said. Indeed, the first letter of *Shema*, the *shin*, has what sound? "Sh"… shhh…quiet…don't speak. Just listen.

2. *Allow the patient to share his or her stories.* Too often, visitors introduce their own stories. They sympathize with what the patient is experiencing, but they do not *empathize.* The visitor mistakenly believes that comparing his or her own illness to that of the patient will forge a bond of understanding.

Quite the contrary – the patient who is suffering and in pain is *not* interested in someone else's tale. It is she who needs comfort, not the visitor. Remember, *bikur cholim* is not about the visitor; it is all about the person being visited.

3. *Help the patient voice his prayer to God.* A patient is often unable to articulate the feelings and emotions he is experiencing. As we begin to actively listen to the stories and hear those pieces he chooses to share with us, a picture begins to evolve: concerns about his age, mortality, health, children, relationships with family, friends – and particularly with God.

Many would like to pray, to dialogue with God, but feel that they lack the tools. Perhaps for personal reasons they feel they are unworthy in God's eyes to speak to Him and to ask for His help. It is in situations such as these that we can be most helpful. In our role as *bikur cholim* caregivers, we can be transformed and become the patient's surrogate – we become his voice and articulate his prayers on his behalf.

Prayer that is created to express a patient's wishes or concerns is known as "spontaneous prayer." How does one who is not a member of the clergy initiate prayer in a natural way? It may require some practice to become proficient at it, but if you follow these three steps, you will find that the patient will appreciate the opportunity for spontaneous prayer: (1) Ask the patient for permission. ("Is it okay to recite a prayer for/with you?") If the answer is yes, (2) ask what he or she would like the prayer to include. (3) With this information, create a simple prayer, such as:

> *May God, Who blessed our ancestors, bless you with healing and health. May He be kind and compassionate to you and fulfill all of your personal prayers for... (enumerate them!) May God give you continued strength and courage to meet the challenge of your illness and grant you a full and complete recovery.*

To pray using a patient's thoughts, emotions, and sometimes his very own words allows him to feel God's presence palpably, to feel that God is truly with him. The visitor's voice can connect the patient to our Creator and be a source of comfort in a time of need.

Chapter Four

What If You Were the Patient?

The lecture hall at the medical school was buzzing with anticipation. The chief of medicine was about to address the first-year medical students. He had an important announcement to make. "I am sorry to tell you that each one of you has been exposed to an illness that we have been unable to diagnose. You will have to be admitted to our hospital for two or three days. During this time, you will undergo a variety of tests, some simple and some slightly invasive. Don't worry – we are certain you will be just fine after your hospital stay."

The medical students were stunned. They had no idea what was going on or why they suddenly had become patients. As planned, each student was admitted to the hospital, diagnosis unknown. Over the next few days, each had his or her blood pressure monitored every four hours. Blood was drawn. Oxygen was administered via a nasal tube. Temperatures, oral and rectal, were taken. Minor digital rectal exams were performed. They were awakened at three o'clock each morning to swallow some pills. They were left on a gurney for an hour, awaiting a chest X-ray. And they were fed hospital meals. As time went on, some of the students became worried, anxiously asking for the results of their tests.

After their discharge, they were gathered into the same lecture hall to be addressed once again by the chief of medicine.

He began speaking slowly. "The good news is that each of you is completely healthy. The other good news is that each of you has passed an experiment which we feel will remain with you forever.

"Medicine is not simply about curing. More importantly, it is also about *caring*. Unless you understand what your patients are going through and experiencing – both physically and emotionally – you will never become a healer. You will always remain only a doctor.

"Over these past few days we have tried to teach you to experience the anxiety and the discomfort of the tests you will someday administer to your patients. Always remember: patients are not numbers on barcodes. They are human beings, God's creations, members of your very own family."

Unless you are able to place yourself into the psychological and emotional state of the person being visited, and identify with him to sense "where he is," it is difficult to "be with him" in his time of distress. Unless you can empathize, you cannot truly feel the concerns he is experiencing.

So to be an effective healer, try to comprehend the nature of the person's emotional state. This may be hard for you. Then again, you may once have been a patient in a hospital. Perhaps you know family or friends who have been hospitalized. Can you recall the emotions and feelings you experienced or were told about by others close to you who had been patients?

Let's make a list and see whether we can isolate and describe just some of the feelings we experienced. In the left-hand column, let's list the negatives. On the right side, we'll list the positives.

NEGATIVES	POSITIVES

Some negative feelings you might have experienced include:

Anxiety	Abandonment
Fear	Loss of self-esteem
Isolation	Expendability
Loneliness	Depression
Denial	Powerlessness
Loss of dignity	Dependency
Helplessness	Anger

Some patients do experience positive feelings during their hospital stay. Let's list these feelings in the right-hand column.

Gratitude – for being in a place where illness can be treated

Appreciation – for the hospital's care

Thankfulness – that a diagnosis can be determined

Hope – for a full recovery

But, by and large, the overwhelming emotions experienced by a patient are the negative ones that we have enumerated. It is these negative emotions that infiltrate our being and become part of us, perhaps causing additional stress to our bodies and even hampering our ability to recover.

Rarely, if ever, will you encounter a patient who is experiencing all of the negative emotions described. However, it is important to realize that every patient experiences emotions somewhere along this spectrum.

Once we internalize these feelings, we are able to connect with the patient, "hear" what she is saying, and validate her feelings. We show her that she is not alone, that it is okay to experience what she is describing. Most importantly, we convey the sense that God has made us all one family and that we truly care about our brothers and sisters.

Chapter Five

A "Virtual" Hospital Visit:

Test Your Instincts for *Bikur Cholim*

Now that we've learned all about the concept of *bikur cholim* visits –
their meaning, purpose, religious and philosophical sources, what we
are expected to do and not to do – it's time to put all of our knowledge
together and embark on a hospital visit.

When you read the following scripted scenario, look carefully
at every action and statement. Had you been the patient yourself,
would you have found this visit meaningful or comforting? Was
anything missing from the visit? Were any mistakes made? As a *bikur
cholim* visitor, what would you do or not do, given the same set of
circumstances?

If you like, you can take a blank sheet of paper and jot down
your impressions of both the positives and negatives of this visit. See
what you discover on your own. I promise it will be an interesting
journey.

When you have finished, we will review together, step by step,
the actions taken and see what lessons we can learn. Hopefully, after
we have analyzed each action, we also will have formulated specific
guidelines to making an effective and helpful *bikur cholim* visit.

Remember, these suggestions and directives are not written in stone. It is perfectly acceptable to be flexible in their use and certainly to be creative in your role as a visitor.

Joan's Bikur Cholim *Hospital Visit*

Joan and Marilyn are very good friends. Although they try to speak to one another daily, it's been two days since there's been any communication.

While shopping in a local supermarket, Joan hears through the grapevine that two days ago, Marilyn's eighty-four-year-old mother, who lives in Cincinnati and was visiting for the week, had to be rushed to the hospital – something about difficulty breathing…water on the lungs…congestive heart failure. Marilyn, she is told, has remained with her mother at the hospital constantly for the past two days.

Joan immediately rearranges her schedule. She buys some flowers, chocolates, and a large container of fresh chicken soup, a food she's certain Marilyn's mother loves! Then she quickly drives to the hospital to see what she can do to help.

Upon her arrival at the hospital, Joan asks for directions to the mother's room. She is told that it is a semi-private room and that the other patient is a sixty-seven-year-old female named Maria Gonzalez-Lopez. Before getting into the elevator, Joan freshens up her makeup with lipstick, eye shadow, and blush. A quick spray of perfume, and she's ready to visit.

Arriving on the fifth floor, Joan exits the elevator and quickly finds Room 514. The door is open and she enters, noticing that the patient nearest the door is sleeping. Across the room, she sees Marilyn sitting in an armchair next to her mother's bed. Marilyn's mother is awake, but appears tired. She has an IV in her arm and an oxygen mask covers her nose and mouth. Her hair is disheveled and her complexion is pale. Her hospital gown is soiled and ill-fitting.

An unopened gift-wrapped bowl of fruit and a bouquet of flowers sit on the windowsill, next to a family photograph with pictures of four adults and seven children. A sign, written in a childish script, says, "Get well, Grandma – We love you!"

Joan rushes over to Marilyn. "Marilyn, what's going on?" she asks loudly. "I was so worried about you! I didn't hear from you for two days and then I heard that your mother was not well, that she was in the hospital, she couldn't breathe and has heart problems. I'm so glad to see both of you!"

A strange look crosses Marilyn's face. Is it sadness? Annoyance? Anger? She doesn't answer Joan's greeting. Without waiting for a response, Joan turns, walks over to Marilyn's mother's bed, and says, "I know how you must feel. I was in the hospital myself a year ago and it wasn't a great experience. I was so sick and in such pain! But don't worry. You look fine and I'm sure you've got wonderful doctors and you'll be okay real soon – I promise. Just think positively and you'll be home in a few days. I hope they're giving you Lasix to help get rid of the water in your system. Anyway, I brought you some 'Jewish penicillin,' fresh chicken soup – the kind you love. It's guaranteed to make you feel better!" Joan leans over the bed and takes both of Marilyn's mother's hands in hers, gives her a big kiss, and again says, "Don't worry; you'll be fine real soon."

Joan continues to talk to Marilyn, who has moved across the room, away from her mother's bedside. Marilyn looks sad and pensive as she stares blankly out the window. To make her feel better, Joan fills the room with talk about the news of the neighborhood.

Marilyn responds occasionally, but really doesn't seem too interested in the whole conversation.

After about thirty-five minutes, Joan says that she must get ready to go. She promises to call and come again. "If there's anything you need, please let me know and I'll take care of it for you," she says. She gives Marilyn and her mother a warm squeeze and says, "Goodbye, I hope you'll feel better real soon."

She leaves the room slowly, passing Mrs. Gonzalez, who is sitting up in her bed. She smiles at Joan as their eyes meet. Joan quickly exits the room and returns home.

After preparing dinner, Joan calls a few of her friends to let them know about the seriousness of Marilyn's mother's condition. She suggests they spread the word so that Marilyn and her mother can be kept in everyone's prayers. Joan goes to sleep happy in the knowledge that she has been able to perform the *mitzvah* of *bikur cholim* for Marilyn and her dear mother. After all, what are friends for?

Chapter Six

Before You Walk in the Door:

Guidelines 1–4

Well, you've just observed a hospital visit. Did you jot down the things that looked just fine – things that perhaps you yourself would have done? How many were there? What about the actions that Joan took that you felt were wrong or improper? Perhaps you felt that the entire visit was flawed, that it was completely improper and not a very good example of what *bikur cholim* is all about. Or perhaps you felt that it was excellent, and that you would have acted just as Joan did in every aspect. Let's review the entire visit slowly, point by point, to see what lessons can be learned.

Before we begin, there is one critical point that has to be made: anyone involved in the noble *mitzvah* of *bikur cholim* is always well intentioned. At no time should we ever view visitors' actions in any other way. Though sometimes incorrect, their efforts always are, nonetheless, sincere expressions of their concern for the benefit and well-being of the person they are visiting. My ultimate goal is to make certain that visitors maximize their important role as caregivers and messengers of *chesed* (kindness).

Now let's analyze the scripted scenario one point at a time.

> *Joan and Marilyn are very good friends. Although they try to speak to one another daily, it's been two days since there's been any communication.*
>
> *While shopping in a local supermarket, Joan hears through the grapevine that two days ago, Marilyn's eighty-four-year-old mother, who lives in Cincinnati and was visiting for the week, had to be rushed to the hospital – something about difficulty breathing...water on the lungs...congestive heart failure. Marilyn, she is told, has remained with her mother at the hospital constantly for the past two days.*

The paragraphs above are simply factual. They describe the close friendship between Joan and Marilyn and the disturbing information about Marilyn's mother that Joan has just heard.

> *Joan immediately rearranges her schedule. She buys some flowers, chocolates, and a large container of fresh chicken soup, a food she's certain Marilyn's mother loves! Then she quickly drives to the hospital to see what she can do to help.*

The story begins to detail the closeness of Joan's relationship to Marilyn. What a special friend she seems to be. Showing no concern for herself, she immediately rearranges her busy schedule, drops everything she had planned for the day, quickly purchases a favorite chicken soup for Marilyn's mother, and runs off to the hospital to be with Marilyn and her mother. What a wonderful, caring, and loyal friend – or is she?

GUIDELINE #1: *Always call before visiting to see if it is okay to visit.*

Does Joan know whether Marilyn or her mother is in the mood for company at this time? Does she know if Marilyn's mother is in pain or distress and may not want visitors to disturb her? Isn't it possible that Marilyn's mother prefers privacy and quiet and just wants to be left alone for now? In fact, as we shall soon learn, Marilyn's mother is tired, looks unkempt and disheveled, is wearing a soiled and ill-fitting gown, and has an oxygen mask covering her face. If you were the patient, would you want a surprise visit, no matter how well intentioned, even from a close friend, under these circumstances?

A true story: Many years ago, the wife of a longtime dear friend of mine was diagnosed with advanced liver cancer. She was also a close friend – an educated, elegant woman with a warm and engaging personality, outgoing and friendly. Her husband, by contrast, was more reserved by nature, somewhat of an introvert. He did not have as many friends because his personality was more distant. But he was a loving, loyal, and devoted soul mate. Both of them were extremely private people and very few of their friends could penetrate their privacy.

When she became ill a few years earlier, I was one of the few people she would allow to visit her in her well-appointed, upscale apartment. Her illness progressed and it was clear that she was fast becoming terminally ill. I was told that she had been admitted to the hospital and wanted no visitors except family – no exceptions. I had no intention of violating her wishes but felt that a visit to the family, especially to my friend, who I knew was suffering emotionally, would certainly be welcomed and appreciated.

When I stepped off the elevator and entered the visitors' waiting room, I saw my friend and his children sitting together, by themselves. The icy stare and cold reception I received almost sent a chill down my spine. Never had I expected such a "welcome." Within thirty seconds, I found myself going down in the elevator to the refuge of the street. I obviously had done something wrong, but at that time, I had no idea what it was.

Many years later (I had already received my degree in chaplaincy training and had become board certified as a hospital chaplain) I lectured to a group of people interested in forming a *bikur cholim* group. My friend was among the participants. When I came to the guideline "Always call before visiting," my friend interrupted the lecture and said, "Now you know why I treated you so coldly."

"Yes," I responded. "Now I understand. You were right and I was wrong." But as I uttered those words, I couldn't help but think to myself, "Boy, am I glad you don't carry a grudge!"

Remember, *bikur cholim* is not about you; it is all about the patient and his comfort and his needs. Even though one is well intentioned, the final decision as to whether visitation should occur rests with the patient, not with the visitor.

GUIDELINE #2: *Do not bring any foods to the patient unless you have received authorization from the hospital to do so.*

Joan brings Marilyn's mother chocolates and chicken soup. Although it is definitely not a crime to bring food – the gesture is certainly well meaning – I do not believe it is good judgment to bring certain foods without first determining whether the food or beverage will be harmful to the patient. For example, one should not bring a diabetic patient a box of chocolates, for obvious reasons. Similarly, in our scenario, Marilyn's mother, who is eighty-four years old and is suspected of having difficulty breathing, water on the lungs, and congestive heart failure, certainly should avoid foods with high sodium levels. Chicken soup is probably the worst and most dangerous food for her under these circumstances.

What about eating food that the patient offers to you that was brought to him by other visitors? Though not a specific rule, it is my strong opinion that one should not eat any food that has been in the patient's room for even a short period of time. Hospitals are breeding grounds for a variety of bacteria and germs. Why take a chance and eat something that may be infested? My advice, therefore, is to respectfully decline any food that is offered to you by a patient, regardless of whether he is a friend or even a family member.

Guideline #3: *Do not wear perfume or cologne, even a mildly scented one, when visiting a patient.*

> *Upon her arrival at the hospital, Joan asks for directions to the mother's room. She is told that it is a semi-private room and that the other patient is a sixty-seven-year-old female named Maria Gonzalez-Lopez. Before getting into the elevator, Joan freshens up her makeup with lipstick, eye shadow, and blush. A quick spray of perfume, and she's ready to visit.*

Although one should always be neat and clean, one must also be aware of smells or odors that may make the patient uncomfortable. Patients become highly sensitized to even the most tasteful fragrances and their usage therefore should be avoided while visiting. Plain soap and water are enough. Save the cologne for when the patient is out of the hospital and you are enjoying a social evening together.

Guideline #4: *Do not enter a patient's room before washing your hands; wash again immediately upon leaving.*

When Joan enters the room, she is doing nothing out of the ordinary; she's concerned and anxious to see her friend. Though well meaning, Joan has already "transgressed" a very important rule. It is critical to wash your hands immediately before entering (and after leaving) a patient's room. Statistics continue to show that disease and germs are spread by the simple act of touching more than by any other method!

Most patients' immune systems are already in a compromised state, and touching them with unwashed hands may cause them further harm. Similarly, they also may be harboring a contagious disease, even if that is not the reason for their hospitalization. When you touch a patient, there is a possibility of a reciprocal passing of germs that can harm both of you. For everyone's protection, wash your hands.

Today, most hospitals have wall units containing an alcohol-based sanitizing liquid. It takes very little effort to dispense the solution and rub it thoroughly into your hands. If that is not available, find a restroom and wash your hands there. This small effort will pay large dividends to both the visitor and the patient.

Chapter Seven

Safeguard the Patient's Dignity:

Guidelines 5–10

Now let's look at Joan's actual visit.

> *Arriving on the fifth floor, Joan exits the elevator and quickly*
> *finds Room 514. The door is open and she enters, noticing that*
> *the patient nearest the door is sleeping. Across the room, she*
> *sees Marilyn sitting in an armchair next to her mother's bed.*
> *Marilyn's mother is awake, but appears tired. She has an IV*
> *in her arm and an oxygen mask covers her nose and mouth.*
> *Her hair is disheveled and her complexion is pale. Her hospital*
> *gown is soiled and ill-fitting.*
>
> *An unopened gift-wrapped bowl of fruit and a bouquet of*
> *flowers sit on the windowsill, next to a family photograph with*
> *pictures of four adults and seven children. A sign, written in a*
> *childish script, says, "Get well, Grandma – We love you!"*

GUIDELINE #5: *Always knock on the door and ask*
permission to enter.

It's important to note that not all patients are privileged to have a
private room. In situations where more than one person occupies

the room, the other person may not be of the same faith, color, or race. Recognize and remember that all people are children of God. One should never disregard or disrespect the person occupying the other bed.

Notice that Joan walks straight into room, without knocking. It's important to remember that one of the emotions a patient may be experiencing is a loss of control or helplessness. For the patient, the hospital room is her private space, her domain, her sanctuary – a place where she can, to some degree, exercise a modicum of control. Knocking on the door and requesting permission to enter honors the patient's dignity and restores a sense of control to her troubled life. Give the patient the opportunity to ask "Who is there?"

Here is what I do: I gently knock on the door. If there is no response, I knock a little louder. If there is no answer, I walk in slowly and quietly. The patient might be asleep. Sometimes the bed is empty because the patient has been discharged or has gone for tests. If the person I am visiting is in the bed further from the door, or if there is a curtain drawn between the beds, I knock on the wall or anything nearby to get the patient's attention, and then introduce myself and ask if it is a good time to visit.

GUIDELINE #6: *Introduce yourself fully.*

Once you have been given permission to enter, do so with a smile. Although in the scenario we are reading the visitor already is known to the family and the patient, you may have occasion to visit patients you do not know personally, especially if you are a member of a *bikur cholim* group. Under this circumstance, you would introduce yourself ("Hello, my name is..."), advise the patient which group or organization you represent, and then tell her the purpose of your visit.

Do not ask how the patient is feeling, because obviously, when hospitalized, the answer will most often be "not too good." The best method of describing the purpose for your visit is to say that you want to see how he or she is managing or getting along. An inquiry stated in this manner will probably elicit a more descriptive response.

GUIDELINE #7: *Be sure to inquire if this is a good time for a visit.*

Always ask if now is a good time for you to visit. It is crucial to remember that a *bikur cholim* visit is *always* about the patient and *never* about the visitor. Allow the patient to decide if he is up to having a visitor. And even if he is, does he want to be visited? He may have just returned to his room after undergoing a procedure. He may be tired, uncomfortable, in pain – or simply not in the mood. Whatever the case, it is the patient's prerogative to decide.

If your request to visit is denied, do not take this "rejection" personally. It is not a reflection on you or your abilities. It is simply the patient exercising his right to take control of the conditions around him and restore his sense of independence. A polite response from the visitor, such as, "Thank you for telling me," or "Thanks for your honesty – perhaps another time will be better for you" will be greatly appreciated by the patient.

GUIDELINE #8: *Observe the patient and the room for signs that may tell you about the family or perhaps the patient's religious affiliation.*

One of the most frequent questions that I am asked when I lecture to people who want to create *bikur cholim* visitation groups is "What do we talk about – what are we supposed to say?" I tell them that they should look for clues in the room that may give them a conversational head start. Pictures on the wall, get-well cards, or balloons are ice-breaking opportunities: "Who are those beautiful children in this picture? Who sent you these cards and balloons?"

If there is a *siddur* or Tehillim (book of Psalms) near the patient, you can say, "I see you are saying Tehillim. Do you have a favorite chapter? What message does it bring you?" As a rabbi, I have no trouble asking patients who show no visible signs of observance how they were raised and what observances they may practice. I sometimes suggest to women that they "try" to light Shabbat candles, for it as a wonderful *mitzvah* that takes only a few minutes. I point out that it gives her the opportunity to thank God for all He has done for her and to ask anything from Him. With a male patient, I may ask if he remembers his bar mitzvah, and from there continue to any religious practices of his parents or grandparents. If you are not a rabbi, you may not feel comfortable with this type of conversation. You will have to judge if this is a workable, productive conversation to initiate.

If the room is devoid of any materials, a simple question such as "Tell me where your parents come from" or "Where were you born? How long have you lived here?" certainly can be a conversation opener. As a rule, people like to talk. They want you to listen and to hear their story. So be prepared for an enjoyable and educational journey.

GUIDELINE #9: *When speaking in a patient's room, the tone of your voice should always be soft and gentle – not loud or overly animated.*

> *Joan rushes over to Marilyn. "Marilyn, what's going on?" she asks loudly. "I was so worried about you! I didn't hear from you for two days and then I heard that your mother was not well, that she was in the hospital, she couldn't breathe and has heart problems. I'm so glad to see both of you!"*

Joan literally bursts into the room and, without the least concern for the sleeping patient sharing the room, begins speaking in a loud voice. Joan is careful not to omit the slightest detail that she's heard regarding the reasons for the mother's hospitalization.

Her tone is loud, jarring, and she is speaking nonstop. Many patients are in a somewhat agitated state simply because they are in a hospital, away from home, away from their own beds and their own comfort zone. Their sense of security and serenity has been compromised. They may not be able to express these feelings verbally, but this does not mean that they are not experiencing them. Loud and constant conversation, cross-conversations among visitors, uncontrolled and boisterous laughter, all should be avoided! They are disturbing and unsettling to the patient and can cause harm to her emotional stability.

Sometimes visitors speak in an overly hearty way because they feel it will cheer up the patient. But constant chatter and loud joking simply reveals that the visitor himself may be uncomfortable and feels the need to fill the silence in the room with sound.

Remember that the reasons patients are admitted to hospitals are varied. Some suffer physical ailments while others may be suffering from psychological and/or emotional illness. Regardless of the reason, most patients do not like being in a hospital, and they may be experiencing a wide spectrum of emotions. Though outwardly many patients appear to be calm, they are tense and their nerves are taut. Visitors who talk incessantly and in loud tones only exacerbate their turmoil. Speaking quietly and gently helps to bring a patient much-needed tranquility.

GUIDELINE #10: *Do not talk about the patient's medical condition with others while in the patient's room.*

Joan describes the mother's medical condition in detail while the patient is awake and able to hear every word spoken. Strange as it may seem, many patients do not know or understand why they are in the hospital! Perhaps the family wants to "protect" them from this knowledge, or the medical staff has not yet received conclusive results of tests that were performed. In any event, the diagnosis and discussion of the symptoms should always be left to the medical team to reveal. It is never the visitor's role to convey hearsay or speculation.

There are many reasons that one should refrain from discussing the patient's medical condition in his or her presence:

- As a *bikur cholim* visitor, your function is spiritual, not medical.
- A diagnosis may not have been determined.

- The patient may not have been told the diagnosis by his physician.
- Your input is probably of no value. The advice you may be tempted to offer may be incorrect and, if followed, possibly harmful to the patient.
- The family may not want to discuss the illness with others or have the illness publicized.

Remember that patients who are terminally ill or in a comatose state may still be able to hear what is going on around them, despite appearing oblivious to their surroundings. It is a fact that of the five senses we possess, hearing is the last one lost before death. Consequently, any conversations that take place in the presence of a terminally ill or comatose patient should always be positive in content, providing hope, faith, and encouragement. At no time should details of the sickness or the imminence of death be discussed as though the patient isn't listening.

You've probably noticed by now that many of the guidelines are basic rules of common courtesy. Yet you'd be surprised how many people seem to think that good manners can be suspended in a hospital setting. So keep in mind that behaving in a courteous manner always makes everyone more comfortable.

Chapter Eight

Sensitivity to the Patient and His Family: Guidelines 11–16

GUIDELINE #11: *Remember that often there is more than one real patient.*

Let's take another look at Joan's first encounter with Marilyn.

> *Joan rushes over to Marilyn. "Marilyn, what's going on?" she asks loudly. "I was so worried about you! I didn't hear from you for two days and then I heard that your mother was not well, that she was in the hospital, she couldn't breathe and has heart problems. I'm so glad to see both of you!"*

Joan begins talking to – or at – Marilyn, without once inquiring how Marilyn is coping. Caregivers have a most difficult role to fulfill. On the one hand, they must always be ready to give unconditional support and love to the patient, both physical and emotional. To accomplish this, their attitude must always remain positive despite what they may know about their loved one's prognosis. On the other hand, they too are human beings, and the illness of someone close to them can cause fatigue, burnout, and stress to their bodies. While they are demonstrating strength on the outside, they may be feeling weakness on the inside. For this reason caregivers often unwittingly become patients. They too need a shoulder to lean upon, and an ear to listen to their concerns.

So when visiting the patient who is in the bed, it is also important to recognize and understand that there may be another "patient" as well – the caregiver who is on call 24/7. Talking to the caregiver and inquiring about his or her health and state of mind is an act of kindness that will always be remembered and appreciated.

Instead of making small talk and gossiping about the goings-on in the community, Joan should have immediately asked Marilyn how she was managing, how she was feeling. She did not, and her friend was left with an empty feeling.

> *A strange look crosses Marilyn's face. Is it sadness? Annoyance? Anger? She doesn't answer Joan's greeting. Without waiting for a response, Joan turns, walks over to Marilyn's mother's bed, and says, "I know how you must feel. I was in the hospital myself a year ago and it wasn't a great experience. I was so sick and in such pain! But don't worry. You look fine and I'm sure you've got wonderful doctors and you'll be okay real soon – I promise. Just think positively and you'll be home in a few days."*

Before we continue our analysis of Joan's behavior, we should reflect for a moment on the "strange look" that crosses Marilyn's face. What emotion do you think she was experiencing? Put yourself in Marilyn's place. How would you respond to a good friend who, though well intentioned, burst into your mother's room and simply began speaking nonstop without appearing even remotely interested in you or your feelings? Would you be angry, annoyed, sad? The fact that Marilyn doesn't respond to Joan's greeting certainly seems to say something.

GUIDELINE #12: *Do not stand over the patient.*

Now let's watch Joan in action. She goes to the mother's bed and leans over, speaking to her. If you stand while talking to a patient (or to anyone) you are implying that you do not want to stay very long, and you really want to leave as quickly as possible. A better procedure to follow, once you've introduced yourself and determined that the patient welcomes your visit at this time, is to look for an empty chair (usually already in the room) and pull it up close to the patient's side. Make sure that the patient is comfortable and can see and hear you from this position. Sitting next to a person creates a sense of connectedness and intimacy. It also allows you to touch the patient (hopefully, you have washed your hands), which, for many, is very comforting.

GUIDELINE #13: *You don't know how the patient feels, so don't claim to.*

"I know how you must feel," Joan tells Marilyn's mother. This statement is used too frequently by individuals trying to comfort others. Let's be clear: *No one knows how someone else is feeling.*

When God created humankind (Genesis 1:27), He did so in a miraculous way, for no two individuals were created exactly the same. Just as our physical and genetic makeup belong only to us, so too does our emotional and psychological behavior. We do not necessarily react to situations in the same way others would.

You may think you know how someone else is feeling – you may project your feelings and imagine how you would feel under similar circumstances. But because no two individuals are alike, just as our fingerprints and DNA differ from another person's, it is impossible to "know" what someone else is feeling.

A better conversation starter, one that conveys both caring and empathy and at the same time allows the individual to open up and talk in a cathartic manner, would be, "I remember the pain I felt when I was ill recently. Tell me how *you* are feeling." There is a world of difference between saying "I *know* how you feel" and "Tell me how *you* are feeling." That is because the former statement ends the discussion – i.e., since I know how you feel, there is not much you can tell me. But when you change the sentence to "I remember how I felt...tell me how *you* are feeling," you are opening a dialogue. (In fact, in any conversation, or even an argument, once you say "I *know*..." there is little room for discussion. It is best to say, "This is how I see the problem. How do *you* see it?")

GUIDELINE #14: *Do not dwell upon personal stories of comparable illnesses.*

Joan tells Marilyn's mother about her own hospital experience. Yet more often than not, people who become seriously ill become somewhat self-centered, and they have no interest at all in the fact that you too once had a similar incident. They are focused on their own problem because they have to muster the energy to cope with it. Your previous pain, no matter how severe; your surgery, no matter how painful, does nothing now to alleviate their suffering. It is best to allow them to talk about their illness and to validate their feelings without mentioning similar situations that you may have experienced in the past.

Above, I suggested touching on your own experience to ask about theirs ("I remember the pain I felt when I was ill recently...") but note that it is a passing reference. It is intended to facilitate getting to the important question of how the patient is dealing with his experience.

Guideline #15: *Do not promise what you can't deliver; rather, express hope.*

Joan "promises" that Marilyn's mother will be okay very soon. In an attempt to make a patient feel better, people often promise that everything will end well because we wish it and even prayed to God to make certain it happens. Unfortunately, the reality is that often conditions do not change, and despite all our hopes and prayers, our wishes and dreams, the patient is not cured of his illness. The mission of the *bikur cholim* visitor is not to promise a particular outcome, for we are powerless to deliver it.

We cannot ever promise what the future will actually hold. We are not prophets; we are mortals with finite knowledge and understanding. It is far better to give encouragement to the patient that things will work out positively than to create a false sense of security by promising results that we are unable to deliver.

Our role is to provide hope – hope that the results of the CT and MRI tests will be negative; hope that despite the effects of a stroke the patient will be able to adjust to his new situation and be able to function in a positive way; hope that the patient will be able to resume a normal lifestyle without worry or fear; hope that they will be able to adjust to any conditions that may arise; hope that God will always be with them and will watch over them.

Psalm 27 concludes with the words "Hope in God; be strong and let your heart be valiant, and hope in the Lord." It is our faith in the omnipotence of God that provides us with the trust that despite the current circumstances, things will get better and there will be a rainbow following the darkened sky.

GUIDELINE #16: *Never offer medical advice.*

> *I hope they're giving you Lasix to help get rid of the water in your system.*

The only hope that Joan is offering is that the doctors are giving Marilyn's mother a particular medication. The goal of the doctors, of course, is to provide a cure for the patient's illness. In contrast, the goal of the *bikur cholim* visitor is to provide "healing."

Modern medicine is beginning to recognize and acknowledge the importance of the holistic relationship between the physical and the spiritual in the total healing/curing process. These two goals are both critically important to the well-being of the patient, but they should never be confused: curing relates to the physical, and healing relates to the spiritual. It is critical for us to remember that we must always assign the curing component of illness to the medical profession. It is the spiritual component of the process, which relates not to curing but rather to healing, that belongs to the clergy, chaplains, and *bikur cholim* visitors.

Giving medical advice or opinions is not your role, and the advice may even be incorrect and harmful to the patient.

> *"Anyway, I brought you some 'Jewish penicillin,' fresh chicken soup – the kind you love. It's guaranteed to make you feel better!" Joan leans over the bed and takes both of Marilyn's mother's hands in hers, gives her a big kiss, and again says, "Don't worry; you'll be fine real soon."*

As we mentioned in guideline #2, bringing food to patients can be detrimental to their health. Chicken soup, with its high sodium content, causes fluid retention, which will only exacerbate the mother's condition of congestive heart failure. Lacking any nutritional or medical expertise, Joan should not "guarantee" that it will make her feel better. In fact, it may make her feel worse!

Not only does Joan probably contaminate Marilyn's mother's hands by taking them into her own unwashed hands, she runs the additional risk of infecting her by kissing her.

Kissing can be a wonderful, genuine expression of affection between people. But it should be reserved for the right time and proper place. The mouth, with its mucous membranes and saliva, is a major source of germs, and kissing is the vehicle to spread these germs, particularly to those with a compromised immune system. For this reason, I strongly recommend refraining from kissing the patient or allowing the patient to kiss you in return.

> *Joan continues to talk to Marilyn, who has moved across the room, away from her mother's bedside. Marilyn looks sad and pensive as she stares blankly out the window. To make her*

feel better, Joan fills the room with talk about the news of the neighborhood. Marilyn responds occasionally, but really doesn't seem too interested in the whole conversation.

The *mitzvah* of *bikur cholim* is about comforting, being a caring presence, providing a venue for the patient to express feelings and emotions without any concerns about being judged. But who is the patient? Is it only the person who is lying in bed, or is there someone else who might need a listening ear? As pointed out earlier, the caregiver – a wife, husband, brother, sister, or perhaps a close friend – is frequently under extreme stress. He or she is perhaps equally in need of the time, the care, and the understanding of a *bikur cholim* visitor.

It is clear from Marilyn's reactions and responses that she is deeply concerned about her mother's welfare. She doesn't appear to be herself. She's pensive and removed. Her mind is worried as she stares blankly out of the window – away from her mother's bedside and the reality of her mother's condition.

Unfortunately, Joan responds the way many people do. Rather than deal with the painful emotions that Marilyn would probably want to share with her good friend, Joan ignores the obvious signs and begins to talk about "other things" that she believes will take Marilyn's mind off of her worries. Though well-meaning, she has done a disservice to her friend. Much like a shivah call, when visitors avoid talking about the deceased because they believe it will be too painful for the mourner to discuss, they miss the cathartic opportunity to allow those pent-up emotions to be brought to the surface. Pain – especially emotional pain – is relieved not by suppression, but rather by expression.

What are some of the questions that Joan should have asked? If you were in Marilyn's situation, what would you have wanted to discuss with your best friend?

Another way Joan could have helped Marilyn might have been a gentle offer to stay with the mother for a little while, so Marilyn could take a break. She could have said, "You've been here with your mother constantly. Why don't I stay with her for a short time and you go out for a cup of coffee or something to eat? I'll watch her carefully; she'll be fine. Go ahead, you can use a break!" Marilyn might not take her up on the offer, but then again, she might really welcome it!

As a general rule, in a situation where the caregiver feels comfortable leaving the patient unattended for a brief time, he might even accept the opportunity to go with you for that cup of coffee – so he can discuss the patient's progress out of the patient's earshot, and talk out his own concerns or fears. Your listening ear may be invaluable to him in this time of distress.

Chapter Nine

Important Dos and Don'ts:

Guidelines 17–21

GUIDELINE #17: *In most cases, limit your visit to a maximum of fifteen minutes.*

> *After about thirty-five minutes, Joan says that she must get ready to go. She promises to call and come again. "If there's anything you need, please let me know and I'll take care of it for you," she says. She gives Marilyn and her mother a warm squeeze and says, "Goodbye, I hope you'll feel better real soon."*

Here's something else to think about: If you were feeling sick, would you want to have someone, even your best friend, visit with you for more than a half hour? Visitors sometimes feel that the longer they stay, the more their visit will be appreciated, and the more beneficial it will be.

Experience has taught me that, as a rule, you should limit your visit to a maximum of fifteen minutes. As I've mentioned previously, *bikur cholim* is not about you; it's about the patient. Visits that last more than fifteen minutes often deteriorate into idle talk and gossip.

And while this may be interesting and even temporarily distracting, patients tend to become edgy and nervous after too long a time. They may be uncomfortable because of pain, IV lines, or surgical incisions. Their level of concentration may be compromised. Under these circumstances, patients do not want to be pressured into behaving in a socially acceptable way. They are not in the mood to entertain guests, to answer all their questions or laugh at their jokes. Many times, if given the option, many patients would just like to be left alone. So my advice can be summed up with the acronym KISS – Keep It Short and Simple.

There are exceptions, however. The company of close relatives and close friends may be deeply appreciated, and they should remain for longer periods, provided the patient is up to it. Obviously, if the patient asks for you to remain longer, or you sense that you are not overly taxing the patient, it is permissible to stay longer. You will have to be the judge. But always remember the main principle of a *bikur cholim* visit: it's about the patient's needs and not about yours.

GUIDELINE #18: *Just do it!*

How often has someone said to you, "If there is anything I can do for you, if you need anything at all, just call me." And how many times have you actually taken that person's well-intentioned offer and called? If you are like most people, the answer is never! That is because the offer was too vague, and you were left with the problem of figuring out if the person was sincere and, if so, how the person could be of help to you. They were nice words, but in the end, just words.

Judaism is a religion that requires action. It's not sufficient merely to think about doing good deeds. We must act upon our good intentions; we must transform our good thoughts into positive actions. Yes, it's nice to offer our services to those who are ill and in need of our help, but it is more important that we become proactive and turn our offer into actions. As the famous commercial for Nike products exclaims, "Just Do It!"

There are so many positive actions one can take without being asked. Instead of saying, "Let me know what I can do," offer to:

(1) Make sure the patient's home is cleaned, beds are made, laundry is washed (whether you do this yourself or hire someone).

(2) Water the patient's plants, feed and water their pets.

(3) Stock the refrigerator with essential food products.

(4) Check the residence periodically; pick up mail and newspapers.

(5) Provide transportation to and from the hospital for family members.

(6) Give caregivers some "personal time" to allow them to reenergize themselves.

(7) Make appointments for beauty parlor or spa rejuvenation for family members.

(8) Drive school carpools or help with children's homework.

The list can go on and on, depending on the patient's needs and your time and creativity.

Your kindness and caring will never be forgotten.

GUIDELINE #19: *Recognize and be pleasant to other patients who share the room.*

She leaves the room slowly, passing Mrs. Gonzalez, who is sitting up in her bed and smiling at Joan as their eyes meet.

Our scripted hospital visit scenario intentionally placed Marilyn's mother in a semiprivate room. Maria Gonzalez-Lopez, a non-Jewish, Hispanic woman, is her roommate. Did Joan react to this woman with kindness, with a smile and a sincere question about how she is feeling? Unfortunately, Joan behaves, as many visitors do, with indifference.

Her hasty departure, even as Maria's smile begged for some recognition, showed her lack of concern for another human being. In Joan's defense, one might say that she was uncomfortable with this stranger – she didn't know what to say, what words to use.

Although this might be true, the lesson we should learn is that there is no need for lengthy conversation. How would you feel if *you* were that person and you were ignored? Good manners and ethics should always dictate our behavior. A simple statement such as, "I hope you feel better soon" or "I hope God blesses you with a full recovery" is all that is needed to make the patient feel that she is recognized and cared about by another human being. Sharing your kindness among others, regardless of race or religion, is simply in the spirit of caring for all of God's creations.

I was once told the following story, which illustrates this point well: A funeral procession was proceeding slowly down the main street of a small town. It paused for a moment at a church where many mourners had gathered to pay their final respects. A local rabbi watched as the procession approached him, and as it passed by, he removed his hat as a sign of respect.

Later that day, one of his congregants who had seen him remove his hat asked him why. "Rabbi," he said, "the person who died wasn't even Jewish!"

The rabbi paused for a moment before he replied, "The Torah teaches us that God created mankind – all human beings. Nowhere does it say that God created only the Jewish people! All of God's creations are holy, all carry the Divine spark within them. We must show respect to all people. Moreover, respectful behavior will further the concept of *darchei shalom*, the paths of peace among all people."

Elie Wiesel, the Nobel laureate, historian, philosopher, and chronicler of the infamous crimes against humanity known as the Holocaust, has often said that the opposite of love is not hate, but indifference. It is a "non-action act" of simply not caring, of allowing events to take place without regard to whether they are good or bad, moral or immoral, just or unjust. When one is indifferent, one is emotionally removed from what is taking place.

Unfortunately, in the final analysis, a "non-action act" has a negative effect: it transforms itself into an act of selfishness that is destructive to one's spirit and soul. The *mitzvah* of *bikur cholim* is the opposite of indifference.

GUIDELINE #20: *Say a prayer with/for the patient.*

Joan quickly exits the room and returns home.

But wait – Joan has forgotten one of the most important aspects of a *bikur cholim* visit! It is what distinguishes *bikur cholim* from any type of secular visit. It is the essence and at the very foundation of a *bikur cholim* visit: prayer.

Prayer is an essential component of each and every visit to a patient, whether in a hospital, nursing facility, or at home. Our sages have taught that no *bikur cholim* visit is complete unless some form of prayer is included. The prayer need not be lengthy to be effective, but it certainly should be sincere and heartfelt.

Before praying, however, there are three components that must be considered by the one reciting a prayer on someone else's behalf. The first requirement is for the person to ask the patient a simple question: "May I say a prayer for you?" (If the person refuses your request to pray for him, you might respond, "I hope it's okay with you if I keep you in my personal prayers.")

The second requirement, if the patient answered affirmatively to the first question, is "What is it that you would like to pray for?" The third is for the person to incorporate those wishes into a meaningful prayer. The prayer need not be lengthy and complicated. A simple, short prayer that invokes God's blessings and acknowledges that He is able to fulfill all of one's wishes is adequate. Remember that the heartfelt plea of Moses on behalf of his stricken sister Miriam is a study in sincerity and simplicity: "*El na, refa na lah* – please, dear God, heal her!" (Numbers 12:13).

You could say, "May God bless you with good health and grant you a full and speedy recovery. May He fulfill your personal wishes [enumerate them] and grant you peace. Amen."

Why must you always first ask the patient what he or she wants to pray for? The answer, an experience from my early days as a hospital chaplain, is etched in my memory.

The young girl was no more than eighteen years old. As she approached me in the hospital hallway, she had a frightened and worried look on her face. "Are you the rabbi of the hospital?" she asked.

"Yes," I replied. "Is there something I can do for you?"

She hurriedly explained that her mother had been hit by a car traveling eighty miles per hour. Many of her bones had been broken and she had internal injuries as well. "Will you visit my mother and say a prayer for her?" she asked.

"Of course," I replied. Five minutes later, I faced a woman who was critically injured and whose life was hanging in the balance. We spoke for just a short while; I did not want to add any additional physical stress to her fragile condition.

"Rabbi, will you please say a prayer for me?"

Not hesitating for a moment, I replied, "Of course I will." I asked her to tell me what I should pray for. I fully expected her to say "for my recovery" or "for my pain to be relieved." But her response took me totally by surprise! In my wildest dreams, I would never have expected her request to be so unnerving.

"My dog, Buttercup, died last week," she said. "I know he is in Heaven, but I am afraid that he is not being fed properly or walked daily. Will you please say a prayer for Buttercup?"

It took a degree of originality on my part to create the prayer. But at its conclusion, I saw that the woman's face had relaxed and she was at peace. Mission accomplished!

Had I not asked the critical question of what to pray for, I would have created a spontaneous prayer that was significant to me – but useless to her. The visit would have been about me, about my feeling good about myself and the positive results of my actions. This one question, asked innocently and without any hint as to what her true response would be, transformed my visit with her into a meaningful and lasting experience for both of us.

Now let's talk about prayer itself: Why do people pray? What are they trying to accomplish?

Jewish tradition teaches that we have been created by a Power that is infinite in wisdom and ability, omnipotent and omniscient in relationship to His creations. Because man is a product of this creative process, we must, by necessity, remain finite and limited in our knowledge and capabilities.

Prayer, whether in gratitude or supplication, is the spiritual vehicle we use to reach out to our all-knowing and all-powerful Creator, in the hope – and with the faith – that He will listen and respond to our most deeply felt emotions.

We must remember one critical point: although our prayers are always heard by the Supreme Being, they are not always answered in the way that we would prefer.

A story: A young girl is praying fervently in the synagogue. Her eyes are closed as she sways back and forth, pronouncing each word slowly and carefully. Unable to take her eyes from the girl, a woman waits for her to conclude her prayers and then very delicately approaches her. "I hope you don't mind my asking you, but I was so taken with the sincerity of your prayer. What were you praying for?"

She answers simply, "I was asking God to give me a bicycle for my birthday!"

Two weeks later, the woman sees the young girl walking down the street and asks, "Did God answer your prayer?"

"Yes!" she replies.

"So where is your bicycle?"

"You don't understand. God answered me – but He said no!"

Yes...sometimes, despite our pleas, despite our sincerity, despite our promises to change and be a better person...despite everything, God says no. Only He knows what is truly best for the patient's soul. It is knowledge to which no human can be privy.

A final word about prayer as it relates specifically to those suffering illness. The sages of old composed a beautiful prayer on behalf of those who are ill. We still recite it today. Known simply as *Mi She'beirach*, it asks God to bless and cure the patient for whom we are praying. What is truly interesting is the schematic idea of the prayer itself.

How very wise were the rabbis who penned this prayer: they understood the holistic makeup of human beings, the critical relationship of body and soul. The prayer asks that God grant the patient *refuat hanefesh* and *refuat haguf*, "the healing of the spirit and the healing of the body." How interesting that they first concentrated on the spirit and then on the body. They fathomed the mind-body relationship in the healing process. If one's spirit is healed, if one possesses a positive attitude toward illness and life in general, then healing – though not guaranteed – is somehow easier to attain. Patients who suffer emotionally, whose spirit is broken, whose attitude toward getting better and toward life in general is negative, however, will be less likely to be cured physically. Numerous studies continue to bear out this phenomenon.[1]

---

1. The study of the mind-body connection has become a major area of investigation in hospitals and universities. To name just two: Professor David Felten, head of the Department of Neurobiology and Anatomy at the University of Rochester, discovered "clear evidence that the brain has the ability to send signals to immune-system cells" (Kathy Quinn

In addition to praying with the patient, you can make your *bikur cholim* visit even stronger by including the patient in your own personal prayers.

GUIDELINE #21: *Always maintain confidentiality.*

> *After preparing dinner, Joan calls a few of her friends to let them know about the seriousness of Marilyn's mother's condition. She suggests they spread the word so that Marilyn and her mother can be kept in everyone's prayers. Joan goes to sleep happy in the knowledge that she has been able to perform the mitzvah of bikur cholim on behalf of Marilyn and her dear mother. After all, what are friends for?*

We hope that Joan remembered to wash her hands thoroughly before preparing dinner! Her thoughts are on the *bikur cholim* visit she has just completed. She is truly concerned for the welfare of Marilyn and her elderly mother.

She has already spent more than half an hour at the hospital. She has tried, albeit with idle conversation, to take Marilyn's mind off her

---

Thomas, "The Mind-Body Connection: Granny Was Right, After All," *Rochester Review*, 1997, http://www.rochester.edu/pr/Review/V59N3/feature2.html).

The works of Robert H. Williams of Harvard Medical School reinforce the importance of visiting patients and bringing them hope. He writes in his book *To Live and to Die* (New York: Springer-Verlag, 1973, p. 155), "...many patients have not only physical discomfort but also much emotional upheaval.... A genuine display of interest and determination to help can be very beneficial."

troubles. She has provided "Jewish penicillin" for Marilyn's mother. She has given the best medical advice and has promised the patient that she will be fine. She has instructed Marilyn to call her if she needs anything at all – what more can she do?

Why not bring God and prayer into the equation?

Luckily, Joan is part of a women's prayer group that gathers weekly to recite Tehillim on behalf of people in the community who are ill. She reflects that the magic powers of reciting Tehillim can actually be found in the word *Tehillim* itself! Tehillim also sounds like "to heal 'em!" – to make them better!

And so, with the best of intentions, Joan immediately calls her friends and members of the Tehillim prayer group and tells them all about Marilyn's mother. Hopefully, their collective prayers will be answered and Marilyn's elderly mother will be granted a full and speedy recovery.

Let's examine this last noble act. Joan certainly means well, but does she know that Marilyn wants to make her mother's condition public knowledge? If Marilyn, who is Joan's best friend, didn't call Joan originally, even after two days had gone by, perhaps she had good reason to keep her mother's illness a private matter? Isn't this a family decision? Does Joan have the right to spread the word about Marilyn's mother without first receiving permission from Marilyn to do so? Hasn't Joan, even with good intentions, overstepped her boundaries and violated the protocol of confidentiality?

Anyone who has visited a doctor's office recently knows that one of the forms that require your signature is the one dealing with the HIPAA (Health Insurance Portability and Accountability Act) privacy laws. In a hospital setting, doctors and staff are cautioned not to discuss any patient's case in public places, including elevators.

The fines and penalties for violating the HIPAA laws are severe. In the litigious society in which we live today, we must be careful to exercise great caution in protecting the confidentiality of a patient. The penalties for violating these laws can be quite harsh – and expensive, too.

The lesson that we must learn from this scenario is simple: at no time should we reveal whom we have visited, what was discussed, or what the patient's condition is – to anyone. This includes family and friends. The only exception to this rule would be if the patient himself tells you that it is permissible to include others. Sometimes, patients do want visitors and will not object to others knowing that they are hospitalized. But even under this exception, visitors who are performing the *mitzvah* of *bikur cholim* should be discreet with the information and always remain sensitive to the feelings of the patient. The patient's prognosis, or how the patient is responding to treatment, should not be discussed.

The role of the *bikur cholim* visitor is not to spread gossip but to create an atmosphere of caring, concern, and peace for those who are ill and in need of a warm heart and a nurturing presence.

Chapter Ten

Children and *Bikur Cholim*

Visiting Children Who Are Hospitalized

If you are planning on visiting a hospitalized child, there are many variables that must be considered.

1. *The age of the child.* Infants and preschoolers, regardless of their medical condition or personality traits, probably will be unresponsive to most attempts at conversation. A colorful balloon or two can break the ice. You might consider bringing a book you can read aloud. I know of one case where a toddler who had undergone surgery on her leg was presented with a teddy bear wearing a bandage on his leg, just like hers. The gift was a source of cozy comfort long after the visitor left.

2. *The medical condition of the child.* Children and teenagers who are not seriously ill may welcome a visit and enjoy "small talk," but only for a limited time. Obviously, patients of any age who are seriously ill will be quieter, more introspective, and less anxious to talk, even if their natural personalities are friendly and outgoing. Do not try too hard to change the patient's mood. Instead, be gentle and supportive, expressing hope that the patient will have the strength and ability to deal with his challenges. Avoid platitudes that sound encouraging or promises of healing that are unrealistic.

3.   *The personality of the child.* Children, like adults, may be quiet, bashful, and shy, or open, friendly, and gregarious. It's always best to accept and mirror the child's traits: do not push a shy child to share his feelings with you. You might want to simply ask if there is some particular game or book he would like you to bring on your next visit.

It is my belief that the key to successfully visiting children lies in developing your ability to connect and communicate on whatever level is mutually comfortable. Children are very perceptive. They will not share their concerns or feelings if they sense insincerity in the listener, or even remotely suspect that confidentiality and trust are lacking.

Children are not always willing to open up to strangers. So how does one begin? To help children feel at ease and gain their confidence, I often begin my visit with an engaging riddle or simple magic tricks. (I am somewhat of an amateur magician – not good enough for prime time, as they say, but certainly good enough to bring a smile to a sick child's face.) I then talk with them about themselves and their interests – sports, school, or hobbies.

When visiting an older child or a teen, inquire beforehand whether he or she has any special interest; a fun toy or an interesting game or book will always be greatly appreciated.

Most of the twenty-one guidelines for hospital visits in this book apply to children as well, though several of them are more appropriate to their parents. Remember that visiting children is not a one-dimensional task! When children are patients, especially when they are young, more often than not their parents keep a constant watch.

Consequently, much of your work with children will focus on their parents, as noted in guideline 11, "Remember that often there is more than one real patient." Parents may feel guilty, overwhelmed, and helpless: they are unable to cure the illness or alleviate the pain their child is experiencing. Their bedside vigil leaves them both physically and emotionally fatigued. At this time, parents (and siblings as well) truly need a sincere, attentive "listening ear" from their visitors.

Other guidelines that apply primarily to the parent are:

(#14) Do not dwell upon personal stories of comparable illness.
Every case is unique, and your ineffective tale offers no comfort as parents watch their child suffer.

(#16) Never offer medical advice.
You must let the parents decide what's best for their child. If they seem confused, suggest that they discuss the options with their doctor.

(#18) Just do it!
There are many ways to help the family when parents are busy tending to their sick child. Their other children need attention too! If you can, offer to help with homework, babysit, or take their other children to the park. Carpool help may be necessary, and the family can always use a good meal.

(#20) Say a prayer with/for the patient.
If the parents would find comfort in prayer, offer to pray with them for their child. You may want to add a few words on

their behalf as well – that they should be granted the strength and courage to deal with this challenge.

Above all, during this trying period in the lives of a sick child and his or her parents, the *bikur cholim* visitor can be most helpful not by solving their problems, but simply by being with them as a caring presence – listening, validating their concerns, joining in prayer, and expressing hope that their child will once again enjoy a happy and healthy life.

Children as Visitors

It is my opinion that young children under the age of ten should not visit patients in the hospital who are strangers to them. (Obviously if the patient is a family member or close friend, there certainly can be exceptions to this rule. However, the emotional impact on the child of seeing a loved one looking pale, sick, or connected to numerous monitors should be weighed.) In fact, many hospitals have specific rules about children coming to visit, so you should always check hospital regulations before planning to bring children on a *bikur cholim* visit. Keep in mind as well that hospitals are breeding grounds for infections, and the child's health could be jeopardized. In addition, children are often carriers of disease and the immune systems of patients are often compromised, making them susceptible to infection.

Moreover, a hospital can be emotionally upsetting. There are machines, noises, sights, and smells that may be frightening to a child. Seeing people suffering, patients being wheeled on stretchers, patients with IVs, feeding tubes, or respirators is not easy for anyone, much less a child. Even if the patient you are visiting is in fairly good shape, the child will view other patients along the way. Young children who are uncomfortable in these settings often become noisy and unruly, which is disturbing to the patients as well.

It is true that many *bikur cholim* organizations do include young children in their groups as visitors to patients who are hospitalized, with the good intention of teaching them about the *mitzvah* of *bikur cholim*. Even though it sounds like a right and nice thing to do, I believe young children and the patients are better served when visitation occurs at home, outside the hospital setting.

Summary of Guidelines for Hospital Visits

1. Always call before visiting to see if it is okay to visit.
2. Do not bring any foods to the patient unless you have received authorization from the hospital to do so.
3. Do not wear perfume or cologne, even a mildly scented one, when visiting a patient.
4. Do not enter a patient's room before washing your hands; wash again immediately upon leaving.
5. Always knock on the door and ask permission to enter.
6. Introduce yourself fully.
7. Be sure to inquire if this is a good time for a visit.
8. Observe the patient and the room for signs that may tell you about the family or perhaps the patient's religious affiliation.
9. When speaking in a patient's room, the tone of your voice should always be soft and gentle – not loud or overly animated.
10. Do not talk about the patient's medical condition with others while in the patient's room.
11. Remember that often there is more than one real patient.
12. Do not stand over the patient.
13. You don't know how the patient feels, so don't claim to.
14. Do not dwell upon personal stories of comparable illnesses.
15. Do not promise what you can't deliver; rather, express hope.
16. Never offer medical advice.
17. In most cases, limit your visit to a maximum of fifteen minutes.

18. [When taking care of a patient's needs...] Just do it!
19. Recognize and be pleasant to other patients who share the room.
20. Say a prayer with/for the patient.
21. Always maintain confidentiality.

PART II
VISITING THE
HOMEBOUND ELDERLY

Chapter Eleven

A Special Kind of Visit:
Adapting Guidelines 1–4

The telephone call came from the social worker who was in charge of programming for homebound senior citizens at the Jewish Community Center. Could I please visit Ida Levine, an eighty-six-year-old Holocaust survivor who lives alone in a walk-up apartment in the heart of Manhattan? A brief description and history were given to me along with her phone number and address.

After calling and clarifying who I was and why I wanted to visit, I received her invitation to come over as soon as possible. On the day of the visit I called again to confirm that the time was still convenient. A short time later, I arrived at an old building, found her apartment, and rang the bell. It took about five minutes for her to unlock the multiple locks on the inside of her front door. The door opened just a crack and a little old lady stared at me from inside. After I again explained who I was, she opened the door and motioned for me to enter.

The apartment had a musty smell; it needed to be aired. The living room was small, the furniture old and shabby. She offered me a glass of water – which she served in a *yahrzeit* (memorial) glass, a frugal practice I hadn't seen since my grandmother's day! Though she walked with the help of a walker, she appeared to be in good health and her mind was certainly functioning well for her age.

We talked for a while about her past, and she was able to recall many interesting incidents from her youth. She had never married, and her nieces and nephews had long since passed away or moved to another state. She had no one in her life to care for – and there was no one in her life to care for her.

On the couch next to me was a stuffed animal, a frayed teddy bear. She picked it up and lovingly held it close to her. The next words she spoke pierced my heart – I can still hear them today: "Do you know why I bought this teddy bear? Every night when I go to sleep and every morning when I wake up, I kiss this teddy bear and say to it, 'I love you' – it's the only thing in the world that I have that gives me what I need most…love!"

Not every senior you visit will be as love-starved as that. Some will have family and/or friends who fill their lives with loving care. Yet I have observed that many people, especially when they are old or sick, need more love than they receive. A *bikur cholim* visitor is not going to replace a caring son or daughter, but the comfort such a visitor can give is priceless.

A great deal depends on the condition of the person you are visiting. When discussing *bikur cholim* as it relates specifically to the homebound elderly, there are four basic categories or "levels of health" that apply to the majority of the elderly. They may be:

(1) Both physically and mentally healthy
(2) Physically healthy, but mentally unstable
(3) Physically impaired, but mentally stable
(4) Physically and mentally unstable

Of course, these categories represent a wide spectrum of conditions, and as a rule, none of the elderly experience one extreme or the other; there is a grey area in which many belong. Because they are homebound, the crisis that the elderly experience is usually not physical. More often, the crisis is emotional: they are anxious and fearful. But most of all, they suffer from loneliness. More than anything else, they need the comfort, the caring, and the security of visitors who can talk with them, listen to them, and even show affection in a way that is sincere and respectful.

Although similar in some ways to a hospital visit, the *bikur cholim* visit to an elderly homebound individual has its own set of guidelines.

Many of the guidelines we established for visiting a hospital patient still hold true for the homebound elderly, but some will have to be adapted, and some do not apply at all. Let's compare the similarities and dissimilarities of these two types of visits and craft guidelines for visiting the homebound elderly. We will begin with guidelines 1–4 in this chapter.

GUIDELINE #1: *Call before visiting.*

As in a hospital visit, calling beforehand also applies to visiting the elderly. In this instance, however, the primary reason is to set up an appointment for visiting. Generally speaking, the elderly person is recommended to the *bikur cholim* group by close relatives or friends. As a rule, the elderly are usually in acceptable health and simply need visitors with whom they can communicate. Of course, even after an appointment is arranged, I would suggest that it is advisable to inquire, before you come, if it is still okay to visit at that time. By taking this extra precaution, you can make sure that your visit is still convenient and appropriate.

GUIDELINE #2: *You can bring food, but try to emphasize nutritional value.*

Unlike the hospital visit, bringing food that meets the needs of a homebound individual is a fine idea. There is, however, a small caveat: rather than bringing junk food with little or no nutritional value, try to bring foods that provide healthful benefits. Certainly, if the majority of what is brought is both nutritionally valuable and healthful, a little surprise junk food snack can also be included. Unless one is a severe diabetic, no one has ever died from eating a candy bar!

GUIDELINE #3: *Wearing mild perfume or cologne is fine, unless the person being visited is sensitive to it.*

One should always look and smell clean and fresh when visiting. Unless you are told that the elderly person you will be visiting is sensitive to perfumes, there is nothing wrong with enhancing your presence with a mild perfume or cologne. Often, in excited anticipation of your visit, your host will dress up and use perfume or cologne to freshen up before welcoming you to his or her home. Here is a nice idea: as you progress in your relationship, you might consider bringing a small bottle of his or her favorite fragrance. What a warm and caring gesture that would be – what joy and happiness it would bring!

GUIDELINE #4: *Washing your hands before coming may be advisable, but is not mandatory.*

While cleanliness is certainly appropriate and appreciated, it is not necessary to sanitize yourself prior to visiting the elderly. Granted, their immune systems may be naturally weakened; still, they live in society, one in which most people don't walk around constantly sanitizing their hands and clothing. Using antiseptic is not a requirement. Of course, if there are a number of illnesses going around, it is advisable to wash your hands to protect your elderly friend.

Chapter Twelve

Maintaining Dignity:

Adapting Guidelines 5–10

GUIDELINE #5: *Always knock on the door and show courtesy by waiting patiently for it to be opened.*

Of course, once you've made your appointment to visit, you will ring the bell or knock on the door to let the person know you have arrived. Though the individual is independent and unlike someone who is hospitalized does not need her sense of control restored in this case, show courtesy by waiting patiently once your presence is acknowledged. It may take a while for the individual to walk to the door and unlock it.

GUIDELINE #6: *Introduce yourself briefly to remind the person of your name.*

Your initial "meeting" will probably take place on the telephone. During your conversation, you will have ample opportunity to introduce yourself and answer questions. When you finally do visit the person, a brief hello and a quick reminder of your name will be more than enough to initiate your visit.

Guideline #7: *Be sensitive to how the person is feeling at the moment and leave politely if you discern it is not a good time for a visit.*

It is unnecessary to inquire whether this is a good time when visiting the homebound elderly. The assumption is that you have called in advance and that the person being visited is fully aware that you are coming and is anxious to receive you. If you see, however, that the person is uncomfortable for some reason, keep your visit short and politely suggest that you can come back another time.

Guideline #8: *Observe the room for signs that may tell you about the family or other interests.*

As in a hospital visit, you can look around the room for clues about the family or other interests. But there may be one slight difference: elderly people may have foggy memories. Some elderly people have marvelous long-term recollection, but not short-term; others are just the reverse. It is up to the visitor to "test the waters" to determine the conversation topic most comfortable for the individual.

Guideline #9: *The tone of your voice should be soft and gentle – not loud or overly animated.*

Because being home provides familiarity and a sense of safety, the homebound elderly are usually in a fairly calm and serene state of mind. Soft and gentle tones reinforce this sense of security. There is one important caveat: the elderly may have hearing loss, so while it is recommended to speak gently, make sure that you speak loudly enough for them to hear you.

GUIDELINE #10: *If the person wants to discuss his or her medical condition with you, listen but do not advise.*

The homebound elderly may not be ill. If, however, the individual you are visiting has been ill and is now confined to his home, it is more than likely that he will want to share the story of his illness with someone. As long as you maintain your role as a caring presence and use your skills to listen but *not* advise, it is okay to talk about the person's medical condition.

Chapter Thirteen

Sensitivity to the Person You Are Visiting:

Adapting Guidelines 11–16

GUIDELINE #11: *Be courteous to the person's caregiver and be sensitive to his or her situation.*

Many homebound elderly have paid helpers who spend either days or evenings caring for them. In some instances, full-time helpers are employed. Under either circumstance, "burnout" is not a common problem for professional caregivers of the homebound elderly. Accordingly, the *bikur cholim* visitor need not be concerned with "the other patient" when visiting the homebound elderly. However, if the person has a relative taking care, "burnout" or a sense of being trapped could occur, and you may want to visit briefly with the caregiver.

GUIDELINE #12: *Take a seat near the person to create a caring atmosphere.*

It is obvious that a visitor to the homebound elderly would not stand during the visit. Always take a seat next to or directly opposite the person whom you are addressing. Being in close proximity creates an atmosphere of caring, of wanting to be with the person. As in the hospital visit, this closeness allows you to touch the person in a meaningful gesture of concern, if appropriate.

GUIDELINE #13: *You don't know how the person feels, so don't claim to. Instead, listen and learn.*

Although the setting has changed from the hospital to the home, the rule of not claiming to know how the patient feels remains the same. Moreover, for the most part, the elderly have long and interesting histories to share. There is much wisdom you can glean from them if you just listen.

GUIDELINE #14: *You can tell personal stories of illnesses if you think it would be beneficial.*

The homebound elderly are usually not sick. They generally suffer more from loneliness than from any specific illness. Small talk and hearing about what's going on in the community is enjoyable to them. Because their focus is not on themselves and their problems, they will probably not object to hearing about the illnesses you've experienced. The fact that you conquered your illness gives them hope that, should they become ill, they too will be able to get better. As long as your entire visit is not taken up with illness stories, there is nothing wrong with having it as part of your discussion.

GUIDELINE #15: *Do not promise what you can't deliver; rather, express hope.*

Because the elderly often think about the fact that their lives eventually will come to an end, they are particularly vulnerable to any suggestion that even remotely promises them a specific outcome. As with the hospital patient, the visitor should avoid any promises. Here, too, focus your energies on providing hope that the person will be able to face challenges, hope of being vital and healthy with each passing day. Many seniors may also need reinforcement of their hope of ultimately passing on in peace.

Though the chances that an elderly person will bring up the subject of death may seem remote to you, the fact is that it is on their minds and they may express their concerns to you. Their line of thinking may include questions about whether there is an afterlife, what death feels like, etc., or they may simply want to be assured that all practical matters concerning a funeral and burial will be according to their wishes. As a rabbi, my professional approach is to listen to them carefully and answer their questions along the lines that, according to Jewish tradition, there is definitely an afterlife that is a welcoming, peaceful place – and yes, your loved ones will be waiting for you there when the time comes.

As a volunteer visitor, you may want to deflect this discussion by saying, "I know you're concerned, but try not to worry about it for now..." If they insist on speaking about it, however, either answer their questions as I do (above) or say that you are not qualified to answer those questions...and suggest that they speak to a rabbi. It's fine to discuss practical considerations, but do not make decisions for them or try to influence their decisions. It is best to involve family members in these decisions for many reasons, one of which is to be sure you are not subject to any legal ramifications that could arise based on your advice.

GUIDELINE #16: *Never offer medical advice.*

Hoping to change their circumstances and feel better, the elderly are more likely than younger people to ask for medical advice from virtually anyone. Even if you are a physician, you must be particularly prudent and refrain from giving medical advice, because you may not be aware of the person's entire medical history. Even with the best of intentions, you could mislead the individual and cause harm. If asked what to do about a particular medical problem, inquire, "Have you discussed this with your doctor?" It is important to keep the individual's personal physician in the picture regarding all medical questions.

Chapter Fourteen

Important Dos and Don'ts:

Adapting Guidelines 17–21

GUIDELINE #17: *Let your visit take as long as it needs to be satisfying and encouraging.*

The homebound elderly usually lack companionship and are eager to share the events of their day. Unlike a hospital visit, no time limit should be set, within reason. Enjoy their company, listen to their stories, laugh at their jokes, empathize with their sadness – let them know how truly important they are and how honored you are to be in their company.

GUIDELINE #18: *Just do it!*

The elderly also have many needs. Though care of young children is no longer part of their concerns, they still need a clean house, a refrigerator stocked with food, as well as transportation to and from the doctor's office. Consider helping with any of these necessities. Perhaps the elderly remind you of your own grandparents. Wouldn't you treat them with caring, love, and kindness? Again, don't ask *if* you can help – just do it!

GUIDELINE #19: *Be pleasant to other people who share the living space.*

If there is more than one person sharing the living space, you should always recognize and converse with all of the people present, even though chatting with them was not the main purpose of your visit.

GUIDELINE #20: *If the person is ill, you can wish him or her a speedy recovery; if he or she is not ill, simply extend wishes for a pleasant day.*

Although reciting a short prayer is certainly meaningful, there is no necessity to do so, unless the person is ill. If the person you are visiting is in relatively good health, a prayer may seem out of place. Simply wishing him or her well and extending wishes for a pleasant day should suffice.

GUIDELINE #21: *Always maintain sensitivity to the person's privacy.*

Because the person being visited is not in a hospital setting, the issue of safeguarding confidentiality normally does not arise. Usually, the community is aware of the homebound elderly. In fact, it is often the communal organizations, rabbis, or congregations that initiate the calls requesting visits. The HIPAA laws are not applicable in this situation either. One word of advice: even though confidentiality is not a requirement, sensitivity is. If you choose to discuss your visit with another individual, do so with respect, discretion, and sensitivity. Visits are not intended to provide you with gossip or cocktail party stories. Your visits are the fulfillment of the *mitzvah* to love your friend as yourself: it should always be done with care, love, and respect.

Chapter Fifteen

Children as Visitors to the Elderly

There is no question in my mind concerning the benefits of children, young or teen, visiting the homebound elderly. Should they visit? My answer is a resounding yes! As a rule, elderly people love children. Such visits may stir memories of the past and the feelings of warmth and love they associate with their own families. Although young families may take the presence of small children for granted, keep in mind that many elderly people no longer have occasion to see children on a regular basis. The mere presence of children can bring a smile to the face and a twinkle to the eye of those who are elderly.

What is so wonderful is that the child visitor has no age limitations. Sometimes an infant of just a few months, when carefully held by the elderly, brings immeasurable joy. Because issues of sickness and health are usually of less concern than in a hospital setting, the child visitor is even able to have physical contact with the elderly: a touch of the hand or a gentle hug is so appreciated and welcomed. Accompanied by their parents, children can learn the meaning of *chesed* by bringing flowers, personalized greeting cards, or perhaps pictures they drew especially for their elderly friend. A child who is really outgoing may opt to sing a song or recite a poem, to everyone's delight. (Of course, never push children who are not so inclined to perform, nor to do anything uncomfortable for them when visiting.)

And what a terrific lesson for teenagers! Visiting the elderly provides many learning tools for future generations and demonstrates to them that they are capable of reaching out to others. In the process, they absorb a key lesson: a meaningful life is not self-centered. Young people learn from visiting the elderly that two lives become blessed and the rewards are indescribable. They realize that happiness and contentment are achieved by bringing joy and love to another human being, one of God's precious creations.

Summary of Guidelines for Homebound Elderly Visits

1. Call before visiting.
2. You can bring food, but try to emphasize nutritional value.
3. Wearing mild perfume or cologne is fine, unless the person being visited is sensitive to it.
4. Washing your hands before coming may be advisable, but is not mandatory.
5. Always knock on the door and show courtesy by waiting patiently for it to be opened.
6. Introduce yourself briefly to remind the person of your name.
7. Be sensitive to how the person is feeling at the moment and leave politely if you discern it is not a good time for a visit.
8. Observe the room for signs that may tell you about the family or other interests.
9. The tone of your voice should be soft and gentle – not loud or overly animated.
10. If the person wants to discuss his or her medical condition with you, listen but do not advise.
11. Be courteous to the person's caregiver and be sensitive to his or her situation.
12. Take a seat near the person to create a caring atmosphere.
13. You don't know how the person feels, so don't claim to. Instead, listen and learn.

14. You can tell personal stories of illnesses if you think it would be beneficial.

15. Do not promise what you can't deliver; rather, express hope.

16. Never offer medical advice.

17. Let your visit take as long as it needs to be satisfying and encouraging.

18. [In providing for the needs of the elderly...] Just do it!

19. Be pleasant to other people who share the living space.

20. If the person is ill, you can wish him or her a speedy recovery; if he or she is not ill, simply extend wishes for a pleasant day.

21. Always maintain sensitivity to the person's privacy.

PART III
THE SHIVAH CALL:
A VISITOR'S GUIDE

Chapter Sixteen

The Shivah Call

As difficult as it may be, we must acknowledge at some point in our lives that we are mortal! Though God is infinite and transcends time and space, humans are finite. Our days and years are limited – all of us will someday pass on to another world, another life.

While Judaism recognizes the importance and the sanctity of physical life, it regards death as a natural portal to a totally spiritual existence. The deceased moves on to another dimension that is better suited to his soul, but the family he leaves behind feels bereft. They have "lost" a loved one, for he will no longer be among them. When death occurs, Judaism provides the family with a seven-day period of mourning known as shivah (the Hebrew word itself means the number seven, to connote the seven days), which begins immediately after the burial of the deceased. Shivah is a vehicle to initiate coping with the human sorrow that inevitably follows.

During the shivah period, family, friends, and members of the community visit the mourners in the hope of bringing them some measure of comfort and consolation. This visit has become known as the shivah call.

If you are a regular visitor to a critically ill patient, it is likely that you will get to know the patient's family. You will share with them the ups and downs of the illness, hopefully reinforcing their strength and faith during this ordeal. When it is over, and they reach the final stage of sitting shivah, you will want to offer your condolences.

Visiting a mourner has elements similar to a *bikur cholim* visit, though it is not the same. Whether you are visiting a family you became acquainted with as a hospital visitor or paying a shivah call to friends or family, this section will help you learn the proper guidelines.

The Purpose of Shivah and Current Misconceptions

The shivah call, which is a uniquely Jewish experience, presents an extraordinary opportunity for both the visitor and mourner to join one another in a truly meaningful spiritual healing moment.

The visitor is able to demonstrate a heartfelt sense of caring, love, and empathy, while the mourner is able to use this opportunity as a cathartic release of feelings that need to be expressed rather than repressed. Together they share a kaleidoscope of emotions from sadness, loss, and grief to comfort, solace, and inner peace.

Some visitors imagine that the purpose of the shivah call is to "cheer up" the mourners by distracting them from the reality of death. In fact, the opposite is true: a meaningful shivah visit allows the mourners to confront death, express their feelings, and work through their loss. A person who visits the mourner during shivah should enable that first step toward healing to take place. Sometimes silence is the best vehicle for this kind of sharing.

These guidelines are only a partial remedy. While it is often perceived as a difficult chore, my hope is that with proper knowledge,

information, and instruction, paying a shivah call can be transformed
into a meaningful, worthwhile, and elevating spiritual experience.

What Shivah *Is*, What It Is *Not*

A shivah call *is*:
- Often a highly emotional time for the mourners and the visitors
- Intended to allow the mourners an opportunity to
  - mourn...
  - grieve...
  - remember...
  - laugh...
  - share...
  - feel a sense of caring from friends, family, and community
- Often a time for tears, touching, and for silence
- Always a time to listen

A shivah call is *not*:
- Always comfortable or pleasant for the mourners and visitors
- An excessively lengthy visit
- An occasion for socializing with friends and family
- A time for loud conversation, idle talk, gossip, or frivolity
- An opportunity to discuss business, weather, fashion, sports, or the stock market
- A time for reminiscing about the visitor's own personal losses

Chapter Seventeen

Essential Guidelines: Dos and Don'ts

GUIDELINE #1: *Prior to paying the shivah call, inquire about the meal and prayer service schedules.*

In many places, prayer services are held at the shivah home and the *Mourners' Kaddish* is recited. Inquiring beforehand allows both the mourners and the visitors the opportunity to get the most out of the time they spend together.

GUIDELINE #2: *Enter the residence without knocking on the door or ringing the doorbell.*

The entry door is usually left open so that mourners need not be disturbed as visitors enter and exit. Please remember to turn off your cell phone and other electronic devices before entering the shivah home.

GUIDELINE #3: *Do not bring gifts to the mourners.*

They are not hosting a party.

However, anticipating that mourners may have difficulty preparing meals for the seven-day shivah period, many visitors opt to send or bring food. If you do choose to prepare or send food, specific needs and dietary restrictions should be determined. Under all circumstances, scrupulous attention to the laws of *kashrut* should be observed. Regardless of the observance level of the sender or receiver, confirm that all foods sent to where shivah is being observed are strictly kosher.

GUIDELINE #4: *Upon entering the room where the mourners are seated, try to make eye contact.*

The purpose of your visit is that your presence be recognized and felt. Making eye contact allows this to happen without the need for greeting or introduction.

GUIDELINE #5: *Wait for the mourners to speak first and allow them to set the tone.*

Because a visitor is unaware of the current moods or emotional levels of the mourners, it is insensitive for the visitor to initiate any conversation.

If the mourners choose to talk about their loss, focus the conversation on their feelings, emotions, experiences, and remembrances about the deceased. To encourage such conversation, it is appropriate to make gentle statements such as the following:

"It must be so painful to lose a ____."

"I didn't know your ____. Could you tell me what he/she was like?"

"What will you miss most about ____?"

"Was ____'s passing expected?"

"I hope your _____ didn't suffer during his/her illness."

"When I lost my _____, it was so painful. Tell me what you are feeling."

"Were you with _____ when he/she passed away?"

"Did you have a chance to say goodbye?"

If the answer is "yes" to the last two questions, the mourner may wish to talk about the experience and it is very cathartic. If, in fact, the answer is "no," you can try to alleviate any possible guilt feelings by responding, "Sometimes people wait for family not to be present at their death because they don't want to cause them further pain. It is known that sometimes people can actually 'time' death – in effect, will death to wait until they are ready."

Before leaving, you might conclude:

"I know this must be a most difficult time for you. My thoughts and prayers are with you."

"I'm sure that the wonderful memories you have of _____ will be a source of strength for you during this difficult time."

"There's so little that I can say at this time. Just know that I'm with you."

"Your relationship with _____ was so special. I know you'll never forget him/her."

And, perhaps, as a final comment:

"_____ was a wonderful human being. I will miss him/her tremendously."

GUIDELINE #6: *Upon taking leave of the mourners, face them and recite the traditional blessing.*

הַמָּקוֹם יְנַחֵם אֶתְכֶם בְּתוֹךְ שְׁאָר אֲבֵלֵי צִיּוֹן וִירוּשָׁלָיִם.

HaMakom yenachem etchem b'toch she'ar aveilei Tzion v'Yerushalayim.

May God comfort you among the mourners of Zion and Jerusalem.

Coin boxes or plates for charitable donations are often provided at the place of mourning. It is traditional and appropriate to make a nominal donation in memory of the deceased.

Chapter Eighteen

Special Considerations

Frequently Asked Questions

Q: If the mourner chooses not to speak about the deceased, how should I respond?

A: After an initial attempt to focus the conversation on the deceased, the visitor should not force the issue. The visit should be brief, and words of consolation should be expressed when leaving.

Q: If I visit as a representative of an organization, or have no personal relationship to the mourner or the deceased, what should I say?

A: Identify the organization, adding, "Though I did not know your _____ personally, I want to express our feelings of sorrow on your loss," or "I did not know _____ personally, but want to express my sympathy."

Q: Should infants or young children who are not related to the mourners attend a shivah?

A: If crying or other disruptive behavior might be anticipated, children of any age should not be part of the shivah call.

Q: Is it appropriate to serve food and drinks to those visiting the mourners?

A: The shivah call is not a social visit. Elaborate displays of food and drink encourage lengthy visits and conversations that take away from the focus of the shivah.

Q: Is it appropriate to send gift baskets or floral arrangements?

A: Gift baskets and floral arrangements create an air of celebration and festivity that contradicts the solemnity of the mourning period; this should be avoided.

When the Death Is Especially Painful to Mourners

All deaths are sad, but some deaths are tragic. When someone who has lived a long, fruitful, and meaningful life passes on, we consider it part of the natural order of the life cycle. But when death occurs prematurely – to an infant or through a suicide, sudden illness, or untimely accident – the sadness, the grief, and the shock are overwhelming.

Initially, there are no words that will comfort the mourners. Most often, pronouncements such as "the deceased is with God" or that he or she "is in a better place" or "at least no longer suffering" fall on deaf ears. They sound like platitudes stated to comfort the visitor, not the mourner. At times such as these, all we can do is to be with people as they mourn. Sit with them, listen to them, hold their hands, cry with them…and remain silent. Your mere presence is the best present you can give to them at this time.

There will be occasions, as the mourning period progresses, when you will be able to talk with the mourners about their tragic loss. For now, the sound of silence is the one that should be practiced and heard above all.

A Final Note to the Visitor

In the merit of having performed this act of kindness, the selfless *mitzvah* of comforting mourners, may God bless you, your family, and loved ones with physical health, spiritual tranquility, fulfillment, and peace.

Summary of Guidelines for a Shivah Call

1. Prior to paying the shivah call, inquire about the meal and prayer service schedules.
2. Enter the residence without knocking on the door or ringing the doorbell.
3. Do not bring gifts to the mourners.
4. Upon entering the room where the mourners are seated, try to make eye contact.
5. Wait for the mourners to speak first and allow them to set the tone.
6. Upon taking leave of the mourners, face them and recite the traditional blessing.

Afterword

Our journey together is ending, but yours is just beginning. You are about to embark on a sacred mission of caring, love, and compassion – hopefully armed with some newfound knowledge and insights that you have gained from the pages of this book.

The age-old adage "It is better to give than to receive" undoubtedly has its origins and foundations in the *mitzvot* of *bikur cholim* and comforting mourners. All human beings are creations of the all-knowing and all-powerful Creator, and just as we are physically different from one another, we are also spiritually different. Our emotions and feelings are personal and subjective and they dictate a broad spectrum of human behavior.

There may be moments, even days, when we are feeling down, and a dark cloud seems to be hovering over our spirits. But there is an antidote for these trying times. Remember those who are less fortunate, those whose health has been compromised, those who are without family and friends to buoy their broken hearts and saddened spirits.

At times such as these, pick up this book and reread its pages: find within it the inspiration and the techniques to unlock the injured heart – for when you comfort the heart and bring healing to the soul of someone else, you become uplifted once again.

In the merit of performing these *mitzvot*, may God bless you with many years of physical health, spiritual tranquility, contentment, and peace.

Chazak Ve'ematz
Be strong and courageous!

Appendix I

Sources for the *Mitzvah* of *Bikur Cholim*

In the Bible, Joseph is told, "*Hinei avicha choleh* – Behold, your father Jacob has become ill" (Genesis 48:1). The numerical value of the first Hebrew word in this expression, *hinei* (behold), is 60 (*hay* = 5 + *nun* = 50 + *hay* = 5). Joseph immediately goes to visit his ailing father and the very next Biblical verse states that Jacob immediately became strong and sat up *al ha'mitah* (on the bed). The numerical value of *ha'mitah* (the bed) is 59 (*hay* = 5 + *mem* = 40 + *tet* = 9 + *hay* = 5).

From this event, the Talmud in Nedarim 39b derives the following lesson: those who perform the *mitzvah* of *bikur cholim* are truly blessed because they take away one sixtieth of the sickness. The Talmud has provided more than just a clever numbers game. The sages are telling us that, somehow, visiting a sick person results in at least a fraction of a physical cure. So there is practical benefit to the patient.

Yet there is also spiritual gain for the visitor. As mentioned above, the Talmud elsewhere delineates nine acts of kindness that promise "dividends in this world while retaining the original principal in the afterlife." Perhaps this promise of future reward is in and of itself sufficient reason to act in a selfless and benevolent manner toward one's fellow man. But Maimonides, the twelfth-century philosopher and author of the monumental code of laws *Mishneh Torah*, expounds further on this premise. He seems to reason that one cannot justify the performance of a *mitzvah* expressly for personal reward that is promised to the individual. Indeed, we are admonished in Ethics of the Fathers (1:3) to serve our Master for the express purpose of recognizing Him as our Creator, and to be in awe of Him, but certainly not for any possible reward that may benefit us.

Maimonides suggests that just as God looks after all of His creations, so too must man emulate God's ways and be responsible for taking care of his fellow man. He posits that *bikur cholim* is actually an extension of the Torah principle "[And] you should love your neighbor as yourself" (Leviticus 19:18). It is therefore incumbent upon all people, both male and female, to perform this act of compassion for reasons that are not purely personal or self-indulgent.

There is another Biblical passage that is often referred to as the source for this *mitzvah*. In Genesis 18:1–2, we learn how God visited Abraham, who was convalescing from the circumcision that God had commanded him to perform on himself. It is the third day, the most painful in the recovery period. God appears to Abraham, as the commentaries explain, to bring him comfort in his illness.

Let us examine the source and its exact wording: "And God appeared to him [Abraham] in the plains of Mamre, and he was sitting at the opening of the tent in the heat of the day." It is the next sentence, however, that perhaps is the most interesting, mystifying, and intriguing: "And he [Abraham] raised his eyes and he saw from afar three men standing in the distance, and he ran to meet them and prostrated himself on the ground in front of them."

What a strange and almost unbelievable turn of events! Abraham is ninety-nine years old, it is the third day after his circumcision, it is the heat of the day, and yet – what does he do? He runs a distance to greet three strangers, and upon reaching them, he prostrates himself fully on the ground! The question is obvious: From where did he get his strength? How was Abraham able to act in a way that even younger and healthier men would be unable to manage?

The answer must somehow be connected to the very first sentence: God's visit with Abraham. Yet this, too, presents some very interesting and perplexing questions. Granted, God visited Abraham to ease his pain, but nowhere is it recorded – even in a minor way – exactly what it was that God actually did or said to Abraham! And yet, Abraham was able to gather his strength and run to meet and greet these three strangers!

There can be only one answer as to what God did or said, and the answer – as shocking as it may seem – is simple: God *did* nothing! He was just *with* Abraham in his time of trouble and pain. God provided what is called "a caring presence." There was no need to speak, no need to do…just the sincere and simple act of sitting by someone's side, sometimes in complete and total silence, perhaps with a soft and gentle touch. Just being there is all that was needed to bring comfort, solace, and strength to Abraham – and, by extension, to all of God's creations who are ill and suffering.

There is yet another fascinating aspect to the first sentence that describes God appearing to Abraham as he sat at the door of his tent. At the very end of that sentence, the Torah carefully concludes with two words: *k'chom hayom*, normally translated "in the heat of the day." This detail is intended to set the scene, and perhaps allow the reader to feel the discomfort that Abraham is experiencing.

However, if we read the Hebrew closely, paying attention to the grammar, there is a problem with the grammatical construction

of this statement. In Hebrew, the word for "in" is the letter *bet* –
pronounced *"buh"*– at the beginning of a word. So if the Torah
wanted to tell us that Abraham was sitting *in* the heat of the day, the
last two words would have been written *b'chom hayom*. Instead, the
Torah uses another letter, a *kaf*, a prefix meaning "as." It appears that
the Torah is saying that Abraham was sitting *k'chom hayom, as* the
heat of the day.

What does that mean? It's a very strange construct. It appears to
make no sense from either a literary or a grammatical perspective.

I would suggest, however, that there is much wisdom in the way
the Torah has formulated this verse. Let us revisit the first sentence
with a slightly different interpretation. Instead of saying that "God
appeared to Abraham in the plains of Mamre, and he [Abraham]
was sitting at the opening of the tent in the heat of the day," let us
reinterpret the sentence as follows: "And God appeared to Abraham
in the plains of Mamre," *v'Hu yoshev*, "and He [not Abraham, but
God Himself] was sitting at the opening of the tent," saying nothing,
doing nothing, just being a caring presence. He, God Himself, was
acting *k'chom hayom*, i.e., in his relationship with Abraham God was
being as the heat of the day. As the sun radiates warmth and energy,
bringing comfort and vitality to all that it touches, it also provides
renewed vigor and healing those who are ill and in distress.

And so God, by acting as the warmth of the sun itself, infused
into Abraham the strength and the energy he needed to reach out to
those three strangers who were, according to the Torah, three angels,
and themselves messengers of God.

Appendix II

A Response to Those Who
Feel Abandoned by God

He will call upon Me and I will answer him; I am with him in time of trouble... (Psalms 91:15)

God is with me; I have no fear... (Psalms 118:6)

[For] God will not forsake His people... (Psalms 94:14)

Jewish liturgy is replete with declarations that promise God's involvement, protection, caring, and love for His people – and indeed, for all mankind. And yet, when individuals become ill and begin to pray fervently to God asking Him for His intervention, for His help and His compassion, they often experience the feeling that God is not listening to their prayers. "Where," they ask, "is God? Why doesn't He listen to me? Why doesn't He answer my prayers? Why has He abandoned me?"

Even though, as noted previously, God sometimes says no to our requests, as His children, we expect and hope that His response will always be positive and reassuring.

Before we assume that God is insensitive or inattentive to our prayers, let's first examine our beliefs about Him and our relationship with Him.

Our tradition teaches that God is both *Avinu* and *Malkeinu* – our Father and our King. We assume that in this dual role, whether as Father to His children or as King to His loyal subjects, He will always be aware of our presence and concerned with our destiny. To assume otherwise (i.e., that He does not care about each of us individually or that He has somehow abandoned us) would contradict our faith and lead to a false conclusion.

So where *is* God when we call upon Him and He doesn't seem to hear us? Where is He when we need Him most?

Perhaps the answer can be found within the Scriptures that describe God's relationship to His creations during those times that they are suffering at His Hands. In Deuteronomy 31:18, God warns, "And I will surely conceal My face from them on that day," while the prophet Isaiah declares, "His wrath has not ceased, yet His Hand is still outstretched" (5: 25).

Let's see if we can find a relationship, a common denominator, between these two Biblical statements that perhaps will give us some insight and perhaps even an answer to the question we have posed.

Consider this scenario: Jacob and David are good friends. One day, they are facing each other as they talk and a disagreement suddenly flares up between them. In the heat of the moment, Jacob says that he does not even want to look at David anymore. Reacting instinctively, both Jacob and David immediately turn their backs to each other. As a result, neither one can see the other.

But there is another way Jacob's desire not to see David could have been fulfilled. If they remained facing each other, but David were to stretch out his hand to cover Jacob's eyes, Jacob would then be unable to see David. And because he could not see David, Jacob might assume that David is unable to see him as well. In actuality, David *never* loses sight of Jacob – it is only Jacob who loses sight of David.

Perhaps this is the thread that connects both Biblical passages. In effect, it is as though God declares to His people: *There will be times when I will hide My Face from you and you will be unable to see Me – but that is only because I have stretched out My Hand and covered your eyes. You, my precious people, will not be able to see Me, but I promise that I will always continue to see you! For I am your God, your Creator, your King, and your Father, and I will never forsake My covenant with you, even during those times when My Presence seems to be hidden from your view.*

When we are afflicted, we may be overwhelmed by anger and fail to see God's presence in our lives. In his book *Making Sense of Suffering: A Jewish Approach*,[1] Rabbi Yitzchok Kirzner deals with this issue at length. He offers the following advice, which is both practical and consoling.

> *While it is natural, when caught up in pain, to be beset by doubts, our questions of faith do not have to be questions against G-d. They can be questions to G-d. We can take all the pain and all the anger and cry out, "It is not that I do not believe in You, but You have made it so hard. Please, help me understand why*

---

1. Yitzchok Kirzner, *Making Sense of Suffering: A Jewish Approach* (Brooklyn, NY: Mesorah Publications, 2002), 172–73.

I am living through this. What is this all about?" We can share
our pain with G-d.

When we share our suffering with G-d, we bring Him into
our lives in a way that was not possible so long as everything
was going smoothly. If we open ourselves up to Him, even when
we do not understand what is happening to us, we forge a bond
much deeper than that achievable by intellectual clarity alone.
We build a bond of trust....

Trust is the basis of any true relationship. Were we to relate
to G-d solely through our intellectual comprehension, the
relationship would end each time something was beyond our
understanding. But we are not only intellectual beings, and G-d
seeks more than that we relate to Him through our minds. He
created the world in such a way that we could relate to Him in
all our wondrous complexity.

As a chaplain, I have seen the truth of Rabbi Kirzner's insights
demonstrated time and again in hospital settings. If we have faith
and trust in God, then even in those moments when we question
His whereabouts, we remain confident that He is watching over us,
that His concern and love are not diminished by our inability to find
Him. Secure in the knowledge that God is always with us, we find
peace and renewed strength to deal with our challenges.

About the Author

Rabbi Simeon Schreiber is the founder, director, and lead chaplain of Visiting Chaplain Services, Inc., a not-for-profit agency providing comfort and support to anyone in spiritual or emotional distress. He currently serves as Senior Staff Chaplain at Mount Sinai Medical Center in Miami Beach, Florida, and is the first (ever) chaplain of the Bal Harbour Police Department. He has lectured extensively on guidelines for *bikur cholim* visitation, as well as on the protocols for visiting those who are sitting shivah. He is the author of a well-received pamphlet, "The Shiva Call: A Guide to Comfort the Visitor and the Mourner."

A graduate of Yeshiva College, Rabbi Schreiber received his rabbinic ordination from the Rabbi Isaac Elchanan Theological Seminary of Yeshiva University. He and his wife, Rose, reside in Bal Harbour, Florida. They have five children and many grandchildren.

AIMEE/DARKA   Cell _____

                 Home _____